WOMEN'S RECOVERY

CAPITAL PATHWAYS

Edited by DAVID PATTON
MULKA NISIC

New Central Media,
Sheffield, England

This edition 2025

1

First published in Great Britain by
New Central Media 2025

ISBN: 978-1-917005-72-2

This book is set in Caslon Pro Std

This book is dedicated to all the women who have risen from struggle, woven communities of care, and redefined what recovery can look like—we honour your courage, your voices, and your unwavering strength. May this work stand as a testament to the power of collective healing and the boundless potential of women supporting women.

Disclaimer:

The opinions expressed in the lived experience chapters are solely those of each individual author. NCM is not advocating the use or cessation of any specific recovery approach/medication/spirituality/pathway etc.

Please note also that we have performed minimal editing to the lived experience chapters for them to remain authentic and unsanitised expressions of the authors voice.

Contents

Notes on Contributors

Mulka Nisic

Mulka Nisic is a Research Officer at the Centre for Hate Studies, University of Leicester, Secretary General of the Recovered Users Network (RUN), and Chair of the Global Gender Committee within the World Federation Against Drugs. With decades of active engagement in drug policy and addiction recovery, she has contributed to EU and UN debates within the Civil Society Forum on Drugs (CSFD) and the Vienna NGO Committee on Drugs (VNGOC), advocating for gender-sensitive approaches to drug-related issues. Mulka also serves on the Scientific Advisory Council of the International Society of Substance Use Professionals (ISSUP) and the Global Women's Network. Her current research examines the lived experiences of individuals in recovery and gender-specific recovery pathways across nine European countries, with a focus on recovery capital and the impact of stigma.

Dr David Patton

Dr Patton is an Associate Professor in Criminology at the University of Derby's Social, Cultural and Legal Research Centre. Dr David Patton is an international keynote speaker and his research centres on the lived experience of people recovering from addiction and rehabilitating from offending histories. His research uses the often-marginalised voices of these individuals to co-produce utopian visions of how recovery, the criminal justice system and society can be radically transformed to promote human flourishing.

Caroline Cook

I ended up in prison after years of struggling with addiction, homelessness, and re-offending. After 15 years caught in this cycle, I turned my life around through self-acceptance, stability, and resilience. Now, I share my personal journey to highlight the challenges many face and I work to promote solutions that address the root causes of offending behaviour. I'm passionate about showing that transformation is possible, no matter how tough the road may seem.

Lena Verve

Alcohol dominated my life for over ten years, and I lost my twenties to the bottle, believing there was no way back for me. Now, over two years sober and deeply grateful for the amazing recovery community, I have become the person I was always meant to be. I have my confidence back, my smile back, and most importantly, I am surrounded by an incredibly strong circle of friends and family who support me through my darkest days and cheer me on and lift me up on my brightest days. Their unwavering love and support have driven me to achieve things I once thought were impossible.

After I stopped drinking, I volunteered and worked in recovery services. Being able to give back to the community that saved me and offer hope to those who feel beyond help gave my life purpose again. If I've helped even one person on their journey, it has all been worth it. Today, the future looks bright. I have my dream job - something I wouldn't have without going on the journey that brought me here. I am loved, supported, planning to travel the world, and even working toward buying my own home. All of this was once impossible, and I am forever grateful.

Claire Naughton

Claire finds meaning in sharing her personal journey, hoping to uplift and resonate with others. Through her lived experience of addiction and recovery, she aims to offer hope, insight and encouragement. Claire enjoys spending time in nature and is a big cat lover. Contributing to this collection is a privilege, as she believes every narrative holds the potential to inspire and create change.

Sandra Losty

I am a person in recovery since 1995 and work in community training and education which I love dearly. I am heartened every time I work with a group and see that light go on in their heads that there are other ways and people who will light the way for them. Born and raised in Dublin, Ireland my favourite saying is "*ah shur it'll be grand*" and it usually is :-)

Rubina Khan

Rubina Khan is a resilient individual who has been on a journey of recovery for around 20 years. Her perseverance and strength have shaped her into the person she is today. Rubina is now happily married to an incredibly understanding and amazing husband, who has been a source of support and love in her life. Currently, Rubina is dedicated to supporting individuals in their own recovery, sharing her wisdom and experience to help others on their paths to recovery, Additionally, she is actively working to support people in communities by addressing the barriers to accessing treatment and support services, ensuring that everyone can receive the help they need.

Rae Panache

My name is Rae Panache, I'm a mother of three, and a humanitarian at heart who is passionate about making positive changes in people's lives. I have always been community spirited and meet so many diverse people from all walks of life through voluntary work, community projects and events.

Rita Nangle

I am a woman in recovery. My life is unrecognisable to what it used to be. I am so grateful for all of the amazing people and opportunities that I have had in my recovery. I am grateful to Manja and my auntie Sandra for their mentorship. I have been involved in so many amazing projects celebrating recovery and co-producing new ways to support people who are struggling. I have just set up my own business. I am excited for the future.

Alison Thornhill

I am passionate about everything to do about recovery. I work in recovery services. I have also been involved in a European photovoice exhibition where women in recovery from all over Europe took part. Recovery is contagious.

Tracey Ford

Tracey Ford, based in Sheffield, brings personal lived experience with addiction, both as an individual and as an affected family member. With over 28 years in the addiction and recovery field, she has served as the Chair of the Sheffield Recovery Forum for the past 12 years. Tracey is passionate about ensuring that the voices and experiences of those with lived experience are heard. An avid writer, she shares her journey through her blog, www.haveawordwithyourself.co.uk, and is set to publish her memoir, Blood is Thicker than Alcohol, in September 2025.

Helena Lovel

My life now is truly "*living the dream*". More than I could ever have hoped for 10 years ago. I now live in Sheffield, and I am active in Sheffield Recovery Community. Using my lived experience to support people and services work smarter together. I'm living proof that "*We do Recover*" and when we do, we definitely "*live well better*".

Aliyah Knight

From being a broken, damaged little girl, to a strong and independent woman. Thanks to my trauma. I live a sober and happy life. I have things that no one can take from me again, that's my peace and my power. I have my voice now and I use it every day to share my story and give other suffering women hope. I hope that I am proof that recovery is possible. Healing is an art. It takes time. It takes practice. It takes love.

Jennifer Bryson

My name is Jenny Bryson, I am a person in long-term recovery and for me, this means that I have not used a mind- or mood-altering substance for over 10 years. I am the Deputy CEO of Recovery Connections, a LERO (Lived Experience Recovery Organisation) and I am incredibly proud and grateful to be able to share my journey. I hope it serves as a beacon of hope to those still suffering, even if it touches the life of 1 person then it will have done its job.

Sarah Schonewald

As a woman in recovery, it's a pleasure to get up each day and support people in need. Studying for a master's in public health will give me the tools to help make change on a bigger level. I am so excited that later this year I will be starting my PhD with a view to researching neurodiversity, addiction and vulnerabilities of women in marginalised communities.

Emily Harold

Hi my name is Emily, an almost 40-year-old woman and mother of 4 wonderful boys. And I am in recovery. I have been very fortunate in life, yet I spent the best part of my 20's and 30's on a downward spiral with my relationship with alcohol. I hope my story demonstrates that addiction doesn't discriminate, identifies the link between poor mental health, and helps to break societal stigma and barriers for women experiencing substance use disorder.

Introduction

Mulka Nisic

"My eyes ain't used to these rays. I'm feeling exposed, but I hide no more. I can't hide as the sun shines on all of my glory. My flaws don't look so bad at all. What was I so afraid of? Every part of me is a vision of a portrait... Every part of me is beautiful. And I finally see I'm a work of art. A masterpiece". **(Jazmine Sullivan)**

Recovery is both a personal and social journey - shaped not only by individual resilience but also by systemic barriers and the presence (or absence) of support from family, community, and services. For women, this path is often further complicated by challenges that extend beyond substance use itself. The weight of gender-based violence, the stigma attached to addiction, the pressures of motherhood, and the lack of gender-responsive recovery services often create additional hurdles that make it more difficult to access help and sustain long-term recovery. *Women's Recovery Capital Pathways: Stories of Strength, Overcoming and Resilience* brings together the voices of women who have navigated these complexities, sharing deeply personal accounts of struggle, survival, and transformation. These narratives provide a powerful counterpoint to the narrow stereotypes that too often define women with lived experience of substance use, replacing them with stories of resilience, strength, and empowerment.

This book seeks to illuminate the realities of addiction and recovery for women - exposing the systemic failures that restrict access to support, the stigma that silences them, and the policies that fail to meet their needs. It is both an inspiration and a call to action, providing a platform for women to share their lived experiences while advocating for change. The lived experiences shared in, *Women's Recovery Capital Pathways* challenges the prevailing discourse on addiction, reframing women not as victims of their past but as leaders in their own recovery. It highlights the urgent need for more inclusive, compassionate, and gender-responsive approaches to substance use treatment - approaches that recognise the distinct challenges women face and the strength they bring to their journeys toward healing.

Understanding Women's Recovery Pathways

Recovery is often described as an individual journey, yet for many women, it is deeply shaped by external forces - gendered expectations, societal stigma, trauma, and structural barriers. Gender plays a crucial role in shaping how individuals navigate addiction, treatment, relapse, and long-term recovery. Despite the widespread prevalence of substance use disorders among women, they remain significantly underrepresented in addiction treatment services. In England, for instance, women accounted for less than one-third (32%) of those accessing alcohol and drug treatment in 2023–2024[1] - a disparity reflecting the gendered barriers that prevent many from seeking help. This disparity reflects the unique barriers women face, including mental health issues, caregiving responsibilities, and fear of losing custody of their children, all of which can prevent them from seeking or sustaining engagement with recovery services.[2] Furthermore, research by Grella et al.[3] emphasises that gender

1 Public Health England. (2024). *Adult substance misuse treatment statistics 2023 to 2024: report*

2 Andersson, C., Wincup, E., Best, D., & Irving, J. (2021). Gender and recovery pathways in the UK. *Drugs: Education, Prevention and Policy, 28*(5), 454–464. https://doi.org/10.1080/09687637.2020.1852180

3 Grella, C. E. (2008). From generic to gender-responsive treatment: Changes in social policies, treatment services, and outcomes of women in substance abuse treatment. *Journal of Psychoactive Drugs, 40*(sup5), 327–343. https://doi.org/10.1080/02791072.2008.10400661

not only influences the onset and progression of substance use but also shapes treatment outcomes and long-term recovery success. Addressing these disparities requires gender-responsive services that acknowledge and accommodate the specific needs of women in recovery.[4]

Barriers to Recovery

One of the most critical challenges is the prevalence of untreated mental health issues. Research across multiple countries indicates that while recovery brings significant improvements in work, finances, legal status, and social relationships, gender disparities persist[5] Women are more likely than men to report ongoing mental health concerns, particularly those related to trauma, relationships, and caregiving, while men more frequently cite unmet physical health needs.[2] The intersection of addiction and gender-based violence further complicates recovery. A substantial number of women in recovery have experienced domestic violence or sexual trauma, which exacerbates psychological distress and makes it more difficult to engage in and sustain recovery.[6,7]

Additionally, caregiving responsibilities pose a significant burden, as many women in recovery are primary caregivers for children or dependent family members. The fear of losing custody of their children often deters women from seeking the help they need, leading to delays in accessing treatment or

4 Best, D., Sondhi, A., Brown, L., Nisic, M., Nagelhout, G. E., Martinelli, T., Van de Mheen, D., & Vanderplasschen, W. (2021). The Strengths and Barriers Recovery Scale (SABRS): Relationships matter in building strengths and overcoming barriers. *Frontiers in Psychology, 12*, 919. https://doi.org/10.3389/fpsyg.2021.663447

5 Best, D., & Edwards, M. (2018). International experiences of life in recovery. *Alcohol Treatment Quarterly, 36*(4), 429–436. https://doi.org/10.1080/07347324.2018.1488551

6 *Martinelli TF, Nagelhout GE, Bellaert L, Best D, Vanderplasschen W, van de Mheen D. Comparing three stages of addiction recovery: Long-term recovery and its relation to housing problems, crime, occupation situation, and substance use. Drugs Educ Prev Policy. 2020;27(5):387–396. doi: 10.1080/09687637.2020.1779182*

7 McQuaid, R. J., & Dell, C. (2018). Life in recovery from addiction in Canada: Examining gender pathways with a focus on the female experience. *Alcohol Treatment Quarterly, 36*(4), 499–516. https://doi.org/10.1080/07347324.2018.1502642

reluctance to fully disclose the extent of their struggles.[8]

Stigma remains one of the most significant challenges women face in recovery. Women who use substances often encounter greater social condemnation than men, as addiction is frequently viewed as incompatible with traditional ideals of femininity and motherhood (Lloyd, 2010). Societal expectations place immense pressure on women to be caregivers and moral anchors within their families, making it even more difficult for them to admit to struggling with addiction. The fear of being labeled an "*unfit mother*" or an "*irresponsible woman*" often leads women to delay seeking help or to under-report the severity of their substance use.[6] This stigma extends to healthcare settings, where women in recovery sometimes experience judgment from professionals, further discouraging them from accessing the support they need.[8]

Strengths in Recovery

Despite these barriers, women in recovery develop significant strengths that contribute to long-term stability. Research suggests that women accumulate recovery capital - defined as the personal, social, and community resources available to sustain recovery - at a higher rate than men (Cloud & Granfield, 2008). Women are more likely to prioritise medical care, secure stable housing, and actively engage in family life, all of which provide crucial support structures for sustained recovery.[9] Given the right opportunities, women in recovery reintegrate into their communities in meaningful ways, fostering resilience and social connection.[10]

---

8 Neale J, Tompkins C, Marshall A, Treloar C, Strang J. *Do women with complex alcohol and other drug use histories want women-only residential treatment. Addiction. 2018;113(6):989–997. doi: 10.1111/add.14131.*

9 Best, D., Albertson, K., Irving, J., Lightowlers, C., Mama-Rudd, A., & Chaggar, A. (2020). The UK Life in Recovery Survey 2015: The first national UK survey of addiction recovery experiences.

10 Nisic, M., Best, D., Patton, D., Ford, T., & Heine, S. (2025). What constitutes a women's recovery from addiction? Examining lived experiences and recovery capital of women from diverse European backgrounds. Addiction Research & Theory, 1–18. https://doi.org/10.1080/16066359.2024.2446861

The process of recovery is not only about overcoming substance use but also about rebuilding self-worth, trust, and a sense of purpose. Meaningful social and economic activities play a crucial role in this transformation. Employment, education, and volunteering provide women with financial independence and a sense of identity beyond their past struggles. Women in recovery tend to invest in education and vocational training at higher rates than men, recognizing that economic stability is key to sustaining their progress.[11] However, significant challenges remain, including employment discrimination, gaps in work history, and the need for flexible working conditions to accommodate caregiving responsibilities.[12]

A Call For Change

Understanding the gendered nature of recovery is essential for creating interventions that truly meet women's unique needs - such as trauma-informed care, integrated mental health and addiction treatment, and gender-specific recovery programs. Strong recovery capital, particularly in the form of social support, financial stability, and access to healthcare, is associated with greater long-term recovery success. Recognizing both the strengths and barriers that women face is critical in developing more inclusive and gender-responsive approaches that empower them to rebuild their lives.

This book seeks to contribute to that goal by amplifying the voices of women in recovery - highlighting their challenges, celebrating their successes, and advocating for systemic change that fosters lasting healing and resilience. Their experiences

11 Best, D., Albertson, K., Irving, J., Lightowlers, C., Mama-Rudd, A., & Chaggar, A. (2020). The UK Life in Recovery Survey 2015: The first national UK survey of addiction recovery experiences

12 Cloud, W., & Granfield, R. (2008). Conceptualizing recovery capital: Expansion of a theoretical construct. *Substance Use & Misuse, 43*(12-13), 1971–1986. https://doi.org/10.1080/10826080802289762

offer an unfiltered look into the realities of addiction and recovery, revealing the barriers they have overcome and the paths they have forged toward healing. The women in this collection come from different backgrounds, yet their narratives share common themes. Many women in recovery have not only battled addiction but also fought against the stigma surrounding it - facing judgment from professionals, communities, and even those closest to them. Systemic failures often made their recovery harder, not easier. And yet, they persisted.

This collection of chapters challenges the traditional narratives of addiction and recovery, which too often ignore the gendered dimensions of substance use. For these women, recovery is not just about abstaining from substances - it is about reclaiming trust in themselves and others, restoring lost identities, finding new sources of purpose and connection, and learning to live in a society that too often marginalizes those with addiction histories.

Beyond being a collection of personal testimonies as it tells a bigger story and therefore this book is a call for change. It challenges the narrative around addiction and recovery, shifting the focus from stigma and shame to celebration of recovery, resilience and empowerment. Recovery is not a moral failing; it is a complex, multifaceted journey that deserves recognition, compassion, and systemic transformation. The women in these pages are not just survivors; they are leaders, advocates, and inspirations, illuminating the path for those still navigating their own recovery.

This book is for anyone who has been touched by addiction -those in recovery, those who support them, and those working within addiction services. They offer crucial insights for policymakers, practitioners, and community leaders striving to create more inclusive and effective support systems. Most importantly, this book is for every woman who has ever felt alone in her struggle. May these voices serve as a reminder: You are not alone. Recovery is possible. And your story, too, deserves to be heard.

The Story Behind the Book: Creating Epistemic Justice

Dr David Patton

Introduction:

"Until the lion learns to write, every story will glorify the hunter."[1] **(Chinua Achebe)**

The central question being posed in this book is: **what helps or hinders women's recovery pathways?** The traditional approach taken when publishing a book on this topic would be to assemble a list of eminent academics and invite them to write a chapter each based on their research area. This book takes a radically different approach. New Central Media is founded on the principle that people with lived experience of addiction recovery are epistemic agents, knowledge producers, and experts in their own right. This initiative challenges the dominant knowledge production system that privileges individuals with formal qualifications, such as PhDs, as the sole authorities on complex social issues. By publishing a "*Women's Book*" authored by those directly affected, New Central Media disrupts epistemic injustice and repositions the voices of the marginalised as central to discourse on recovery and transformation. This chapter outlines the ethos and mission of New Central Media, demonstrating how it aims to disrupt traditional colonial modes of knowledge production and establish a more inclusive epistemic space by offering a new approach as to how knowledge is created and valued.

1 Achebe, C (1958) Things fall Apart; London: William Heinemann.

Coloniality and the Control of Knowledge

Knowledge production has long been dominated by hierarchies that privilege certain voices while marginalising others. This hierarchy is deeply rooted in coloniality, which extends beyond the historical period of colonialism to encompass the enduring structures, ideologies, and power relations that continue to shape modern societies.[2] Within this framework, expertise is often conferred upon those with formal academic qualifications, while those with lived experience of addiction recovery are positioned as subjects to be studied rather than as knowledge producers in their own right.

Scholars have highlighted how coloniality continues to exert control over knowledge by privileging Eurocentric, positivist paradigms while devaluing alternative epistemologies, including indigenous knowledge systems, oral traditions, and experiential narratives.[3] In the field of addiction and recovery, this manifests in the dominance of medicalised, clinical perspectives that frame substance use primarily as a disorder to be treated, rather than as a complex social, cultural, and structural phenomenon that requires diverse ways of knowing and responding.

As the wisdom and insight of those in recovery are systematically devalued, interventions based on experiential knowledge are frequently excluded from mainstream discourse, reinforcing the notion that only formally credentialed professionals possess authoritative knowledge on recovery. This exclusion reflects a broader form of epistemic injustice, in which certain forms of knowing are devalued while others are upheld as authoritative. Fricker identifies two primary dimensions of epistemic injustice: testimonial injustice, which occurs when someone's knowledge

---

2 Mignolo, W. D. (2011). The Darker Side of Western Modernity: Global Futures, Decolonial Options. Duke University Press. https://doi.org/10.2307/j.ctv125jqbw

3 Dimou, E. Decolonizing Southern Criminology: What Can the "Decolonial Option" Tell Us About Challenging the Modern/Colonial Foundations of Criminology?. Crit Crim 29, 431–450 (2021). https://doi.org/10.1007/s10612-021-09579-9

is disregarded due to prejudice, and hermeneutical injustice, which arises when individuals lack the conceptual resources to make sense of their experiences due to systemic marginalisation.[4] In the context of addiction and recovery, those with lived experience frequently encounter both forms of injustice. Their insights are often dismissed, and their narratives are filtered through institutional frameworks that fail to recognise the full depth of their knowledge. New Central Media seeks to challenge this epistemic hierarchy by positioning individuals with lived experience as epistemic agents and knowledge producers.

The Role of Communities labelled as *"Marginalised and Vulnerable"* in Knowledge Production

The recovery community offer a radical alternative to coloniality's knowledge structures by fostering environments where experiential knowledge is valued and shared. Recovery is not merely an individual process but a collective endeavour rooted in relational transformation, social connection, and mutual support. This aligns with the concept of generative justice, wherein marginalised communities create their own value systems, outside of dominant societal structures, to support healing and transformation.[5]

Those in recovery reject the transactional relationships promoted by colonial and capitalist structures in favour of transformational relationships built on authenticity, solidarity, and collective healing.[6] This shift represents a form of *epistemic resistance*, as individuals reclaim agency over their own narratives and challenge the dominant paradigms that have historically pathologised them.

4 Fricker, Miranda, (2007) Epistemic Injustice: Power and the Ethics of Knowing (Oxford, 2007; online edn, Oxford Academic, 1 Sept., https://doi.org/10.1093/acprof:oso/9780198237907.001.0001

5 Eglash, R. (2016) "An Introduction to Generative Justice." Teknokultura 13(2), 369-404: Dec.

6 *Ginwright, S. (2022), The Four Pivots: Reimagining Justice, Reimagining Ourselves. North Atlantic Books*

Combining Lived Experience and Recovery Capital as a Framework for Understanding Experience

The lived experience authors contributing to this book have engaged with the concept of recovery capital from the research literature to frame and articulate different facets of their recovery journeys which highlights the potency of combining both forms of knowledge – lived experience and academic.

Recovery capital refers to the resources available to individuals to support their recovery.[7] It encompasses personal, social, and community dimensions.[8] This framework is essential for understanding the diverse and intersecting factors that contribute to sustained recovery and personal transformation.

- **Personal Recovery Capital**: This includes an individual's physical and mental health, coping skills, resilience, and motivation to sustain recovery. Lived experience authors highlight how personal agency, self-efficacy, and identity transformation play a critical role in long-term recovery.
- **Social Recovery Capital:** Relationships and social networks are integral to recovery. Supportive peers, mentors, and community groups provide essential encouragement and accountability. Research indicates that strong social recovery capital significantly improves recovery outcomes by reducing isolation and fostering belonging.
- **Community Recovery Capital:** Beyond individual and social factors, community-level resources - such as recovery-friendly employment opportunities, housing stability, and supportive policy environments - are crucial for long-term success. Studies have shown that communities that actively engage in recovery support create more inclusive and sustainable recovery pathways.

7 Cloud, W., & Granfield, R. (2008). Conceptualizing recovery capital: Expansion of a theoretical construct. Substance Use & Misuse, 43(12–13), 1971–1986. https://doi.org/10.1080/10826080802289762

8 Best, D., & Laudet, A. B. (2010). The potential of recovery capital. London: Royal Society for the Arts.

By using the recovery capital framework, lived experience authors articulate the strengths-based nature of recovery, shifting the narrative away from deficit-based models that focus solely on pathology and dysfunction. This approach aligns with the ethos of New Central Media by recognising recovery as a dynamic, holistic, and socially embedded process.

In addition to highlighting the strengths-based nature of recovery, lived experience authors in their chapters have also explored the barriers experienced during their recovery journeys and negative expressions of recovery capital. While recovery capital provides valuable resources, its access and distribution is often unequal, and systemic barriers such as stigma, criminal records, and economic precarity can undermine individuals' ability to access these resources. Negative expressions of social recovery capital, such as relationships that reinforce substance use, violence or exploit vulnerability, also pose challenges. Understanding these complexities enables a more nuanced discussion about recovery as a dynamic, context-dependent process rather than a linear progression.

The Alternative: New Central Media's Ethos and Mission

New Central Media operates on the principle that knowledge is not exclusive to specific groups of people. The approach of New Central Media aligns with broader decolonial efforts to dismantle the lingering effects of coloniality in knowledge production. Instead, it asserts that those who have lived through the realities of addiction and recovery possess profound insights into these experiences - knowledge and insights that should not only be acknowledged but also elevated and remunerated.

One of the fundamental principles of New Central Media is that knowledge production should be an *emancipatory practice*. This means not only amplifying marginalised voices but also ensuring that they are materially supported. By structuring the Women's Book around authors with lived experience and ensuring they are paid for their contributions, New Central Media actively disrupts the traditional structures of knowledge production. By paying contributors, the Women's Book rejects the extractive model in which lived experience is appropriated without compensation. Instead, it affirms the principle that knowledge is a form of labour and that those who generate it deserve to benefit from its dissemination. This is not merely an act of ***inclusion*** but a radical reconfiguration of ***authority*** in knowledge-making. The dominant model often reinforces the idea that those with degrees and institutional affiliations are best equipped to define and interpret social issues. In contrast, New Central Media argues that those who have directly experienced marginalisation have unique epistemic authority that must be recognised on a par with academic expertise.

By centring the voices of those in recovery, this project not only disrupts epistemic injustice but also offers a radical reimagining of what expertise looks and sounds like. The approach described in this chapter is a result of a radical rethinking of authority. It demanded that we move away from colonial frameworks of knowledge and hierarchical privilege. Instead, it liberated the recognition that knowledge is also produced in recovery meetings, in conversations between people who have walked the path of addiction and recovery and emerged with insights that cannot be captured in conventional academic texts.

New Central Media's Women's Book exemplifies an alternative model in which knowledge is generated collectively and ethically by those with lived experience. It is an assertion of epistemic self-determination - a refusal to allow external authorities to dictate how addiction and recovery, should be understood. This model not only challenges existing hierarchies but also expands the possibilities for what counts as legitimate knowledge.

Beyond disrupting epistemic injustice, New Central Media's approach is rooted in the generative potential of recovery communities. The culture of recovery is not simply a response to addiction but a proactive and creative force for healing, liberation, and transformation.[9] New Central Media aligns with this ethos by ensuring that those who contribute to the Women's Book are not simply sharing their stories as an act of charity or rehabilitation but are actively shaping knowledge production on their own terms. This is an enactment of real utopianism, as described by Wright (2009), wherein individuals create tangible, hopeful alternatives to existing structures. The Women's Book is not just a collection of narratives - it is a declaration that those who have been systematically excluded from knowledge systems have the power to define and disseminate their own truths. In this book we get to read the lived experience authors knowledge in their own words, untampered and unadulterated by academics. Without the sanitisation or the reduction of their experiences to a few quotations interspersed in the academic narrative. We get to read their words in their authentic form without the academics framing within conceptual frameworks of "*what the literature says*" on this topic.

In this way, New Central Media contributes to a broader movement of epistemic justice. It aligns with efforts to decolonise knowledge by creating platforms where marginalised perspectives are not simply added to existing structures but are recognised as constitutive of new epistemic paradigms. The Women's Book, then, is not just a project - it is a praxis of disruption, a step towards dismantling the coloniality of knowledge and constructing alternative futures in which lived experience is valued, respected, and central to how we understand the world.

The long-term vision of New Central Media extends beyond the Women's Book. The ultimate goal is to shift dominant narratives and restructure epistemic spaces, so that lived-experience knowledge is not merely included as an afterthought

9 Patton D, Best D, Pula P, Hollandy Y, (2023)The culture of recovery: An antidote to coloniality. Addict Criminol. 2023;6(5):166

but is recognised as foundational to understanding addiction and recovery that promotes policy, practice and social transformation.

Conclusion: Towards a New, Inclusive and Transformative Epistemic Landscape

The exclusion of lived-experience knowledge from dominant epistemic frameworks is not an accident - it is a function of coloniality, which continues to shape how we define expertise, authority, and legitimacy. New Central Media exists to challenge this exclusion, asserting that those with direct experience of addiction and recovery are not only knowers but also creators of knowledge.

By producing a Women's Book authored entirely by individuals with lived experience and ensuring they are compensated for their contributions, New Central Media enacts a radical vision of epistemic justice. It challenges testimonial and hermeneutical injustice, disrupts colonial knowledge hierarchies, and affirms the generative power of recovery communities.

This work aims to create a new centre. It requires a new way of looking at complex social phenomenon and a willingness to embrace new approaches. As Toni Morrison stated:

> *"I stood at the border, stood at the edge and claimed it as central. I claimed it as central, and let the rest of the world move over to where I was."*[10]

This is more than an academic critique or a theoretical intervention- it is a real, tangible effort to reconfigure who gets to speak, who gets to be heard, and who gets to shape the narratives that define our understanding of addiction, recovery,

10 Thepostarchive (2020) Toni Morrison - intro & interview; https://www.youtube.com/watch?v=WoTELoC8Q0M

and transformation. It is not an attempt to dominate or colonise the narrative but rather to expand it. The "*Women's Book*" is just the beginning. This book, along with others in the recovery capital pathways series, serve as tangible manifestations of the commitment to ensuring that those who have historically been marginalised in knowledge systems are able to articulate their own experiences on their own terms so that we may all learn from them. Their knowledge - dynamically created and rooted in lived experiences, resilience, relational engagement and collective healing and transformation - must not only be heard but recognised as essential to the ongoing struggle for justice, liberation, and transformation. Therefore, the challenge before us is to continue expanding these spaces, dismantling epistemic hierarchies, and building a world in which knowledge is truly inclusive, equitable, and transformative.

Turning the Page
A New Chapter of L

Caroline Cook

Introduction

Having navigated some of the darkest moments in my life, I've emerged stronger, more determined, and deeply committed to change - not only for myself but for other women walking a similar path. Today, I am on my recovery journey, free from the grip of addiction and crime, and finally driven by a sense of purpose that once seemed out of reach. This change hasn't been easy, but it has been life-changing. My days are no longer filled with fear or regret; instead, they are shaped by the clarity and confidence that come from building a life rooted in self-acceptance, stability, and resilience.

I have found a profound sense of peace within myself and gained a deeper understanding of who I truly am. Today, I surround myself with people who value the person I have worked hard to become. On challenging days, I remind myself of where I once was - at my lowest, feeling like an empty shell and a nobody - and how far I've come to regain what I thought was lost forever. This includes rebuilding the relationships with my children, which have become a cornerstone of my healing and growth. From feeling purposeless, I now live with a renewed sense of purpose and direction. I hold on to the knowledge that I am loved and that even the hardest moments will not last forever.

As a woman, I know firsthand how trauma, domestic violence, addiction, and crime can combine to create a destructive cycle.

ɹr many women, these interconnected challenges often leave us feeling trapped in cycles of shame, isolation, and low self-worth, where poor decisions and unhealthy coping mechanisms seem like the only way to survive. This cycle can feel impossible to break, but I'm here to tell you it's not.

In 2021, I found myself at my lowest, facing the harsh reality of prison. I had hit rock bottom - no direction, hope, or sense of purpose. In the depths of despair, I began the difficult work of confronting the patterns that had shaped my life. For many women like me, past trauma is often the root cause of the decisions that lead to addiction, crime, and imprisonment. It's not just the events we experience, but how those experiences shape our identities and influence our choices.

Writing this chapter is my way of offering support to those who may be on a similar journey. I hope that by sharing my experiences and insights, I can help others navigate their own path to recovery. If my story can offer hope or guidance to even one person still trapped in the cycle of crisis, addiction, and crime, then my experiences will serve a greater purpose.

Since my release, I've received treatment and interventions that have supported me in my recovery. I've also been able to volunteer with charities within the criminal justice system, which has been transformative. Volunteering has allowed me to rebuild my confidence and reconnect with my authentic self - something addiction had long overshadowed. It's also given me a platform to share my story, contribute ideas for positive change within the criminal justice system, and advocate for the gaps in support that many women face during recovery - a cause I am deeply passionate about.

Barriers

During my recovery journey I have faced many barriers. Being a woman in recovery has also impacted the nature and types of barriers I have encountered.

Childhood Trauma: A Foundation of Fear and Isolation

As a young child I learned early on that home wasn't always a safe place. My childhood was shaped by constant fear and tension. Both my parents were both physically and mentally abusive towards me. My father struggled with alcoholism, and my parent's volatile relationship created a home filled with anger, instability, and violence. My father's anger and my mother's emotional neglect towards me left me feeling small, invisible, lonely, and unwanted.

My father's anger and aggression toward my mother taught me to associate men with fear, control, and the potential for harm. I came to believe that men were inherently unpredictable and that relationships could quickly turn dangerous. This created a deep-seated mistrust that made it difficult for me to feel safe with men, even those who had no intentions of causing harm. I found myself always on guard, afraid that a kind gesture might be followed by anger or that trust would be met with betrayal. In a household where love and affection were never expressed, I grew up feeling disconnected from the world around me.

Putting up walls in Relationships

As a woman, my experiences growing up in a home marked by mistrust and abuse shaped how I approached relationships in adulthood, particularly with men. The early exposure to toxic dynamics left me constantly on guard, feeling I needed to protect myself by keeping an emotional distance or, at times, pushing people away entirely. These walls became my shield against potential pain, yet they also isolated me, making it difficult to connect deeply or allow myself to be vulnerable.

When I did enter relationships, I was always waiting for things to go wrong, questioning motives, and fearing betrayal. The echoes of my mother's experiences haunted me, making it incredibly difficult to be present and trust in any meaningful way. This underlying fear - that I would be hurt, as I had seen her hurt - was a constant barrier. Like many women with histories of trauma, I struggled to believe that I could have a different kind of relationship, one built on trust and respect.

Because of this, I found myself repeatedly drawn to unhealthy relationships. The abuse I endured as a child left a deep mark on my self-worth, making it difficult to believe that I deserved any love or respect. Society often conditions women to believe that love and acceptance are conditional and that we must endure certain hardships to be "*worthy*" of love, especially if we have a history of trauma or low self-esteem. These ingrained beliefs led me to tolerate disrespect, manipulation, and even emotional and physical abuse. I felt trapped in a cycle where each relationship reinforced the idea that I wasn't worthy of anything better.

Mental Health Crisis in Motherhood

Then, at 17, I became a mother, imagining that motherhood would offer me a new foundation, a chance to find purpose and stability. But instead of feeling a natural bond with my baby, I felt detached, almost numb. I didn't want to be near him and didn't know how to care for him in the way a mother "*should*." My depression and anxiety, compounded by unresolved trauma, clouded any sense of connection, leaving me overwhelmed and trapped by expectations I didn't know how to fulfil.

For young mothers struggling with mental health, societal judgment adds yet another layer of pressure. There's an expectation that mothers, regardless of age, should instinctively set their struggles aside for the sake of their children. But depression doesn't simply vanish; it touches every part of life. The guilt of not being the mother I thought I was supposed to be only deepened my feelings of inadequacy. I wanted help but feared the judgment I might face if I reached out, aware of the societal tendency to view struggling young mothers as irresponsible or incapable.

Alcohol and Crime: The Cycle of Self-Destruction

For many women, myself included, alcohol often begins as a means to cope with unresolved emotional pain. Growing up in a chaotic environment shaped by my father's alcoholism and toxic family dynamics, I struggled with self-worth and feelings of inadequacy. In adulthood, I found that alcohol offered an escape, numbing the overwhelming sense of fear, loneliness, and failure that followed me from childhood. Drinking provided temporary relief, allowing me to quiet the anxiety and negative thoughts that seemed constant in my head.

But over time, alcohol became more than just a coping mechanism - it was a tool that fed my self-destructive patterns. Many women who have histories of trauma and neglect can find themselves in similar cycles. But as alcohol numbs the pain, it also fuels the behaviours and relationships that reinforce feelings of unworthiness.

For me, alcohol led to a series of poor decisions that ultimately spiralled into crime. As my drinking intensified, so did my despair, and I began making choices that brought about more trouble and deepened my sense of hopelessness. The consequences of these choices became a revolving door of crisis, addiction, and crime with each bad decision feeding into the next. I felt trapped in this cycle, unable to see a way out.

Over the years, the prison sentences I received did little to help address the root causes of my addiction or the trauma that fuelled it. Instead, I found myself returning to court with my offenses escalating each time. Without trauma-informed care, the criminal justice system often perpetuates the cycle rather than helping to break it. For me, years passed in this relentless loop of anxiety, shame, and the haunting weight of both my past traumas and the damage I had caused.

Homelessness: The Unique Challenges of Living on the Streets as a Woman

Eventually, the consequences of my choices caught up with me. My life had become consumed by alcohol, crime, and relentless waves of depression and anxiety. I lost everything: my children were taken into care, I lost my home and became street homeless.

When I was placed in hostels and various homeless shelters, it became clear that these spaces weren't equipped to address women's unique needs. For many women, living in a shelter filled primarily with men adds layers of vulnerability and fear, and I felt that each day. My anxiety and behaviours, amplified by alcohol, led to conflicts, but much of my defensiveness came from a constant sense of threat. The shelters were crowded with men who, knowingly or unknowingly, encroached on personal boundaries, making me feel perpetually unsafe. Sharing spaces with men heightened my need to be on guard. My lashing out was often a defensive response, an attempt to protect myself in an environment that felt neither welcoming nor safe.

Each time I was forced out of a shelter for reacting to these threats, it deepened my isolation and despair. The streets became my only option, and as a woman alone, I was exposed to dangers that felt overwhelming. There was no privacy, no sense of belonging, and no real support. I was often trying to get arrested as sleeping in a cell felt safer than sleeping in hedges and carparks.

What Supported Me Along My Recovery Pathway

Beginning my recovery journey was a daunting challenge. For so long, I had tried to manage everything on my own, believing that asking for help meant weakness. But healing requires vulnerability, and I soon realised that facing the painful memories I had long tried to bury was impossible without support.

Mental Health Treatment Requirement (MHTR)

In 2021, my journey took a pivotal turn when the court decided to offer me something different - a chance to address the root causes of my re-offending. Instead of more time behind bars, I was allowed to complete a Mental Health Treatment Requirement (MHTR) and the Thinking Skills Programme (TSP) as part of my community sentence. I was relieved by this decision, knowing that something needed to change, and I was determined to engage. Up until that point, nothing else had worked for me, and I was desperate for a path forward.

However, starting treatment was not easy. At first, I hesitated because my psychologist was male. Given my history of trauma and abuse, the idea of opening up to a man felt uncomfortable and triggered deep-rooted fears of vulnerability. I had learned to shield myself from men, having spent so much of my life trying to protect myself from harm. The thought of trusting a man with the most painful parts of my story felt terrifying. I had to push past this fear and recognise that healing required facing uncomfortable truths and situations.

Fortunately, my psychologist was compassionate, empathetic, and understanding. He didn't rush me or push me too hard but instead allowed me to open up at my own pace. His reassurances that my feelings and experiences were valid made me feel seen and heard in a way I hadn't before. This validation was the key that unlocked my ability to confront my mental health issues in a way I never thought possible.

The Thinking Skills Program (TSP)

After I completed the MHTR, I started the Thinking Skills Programme (TSP) which played an important role in teaching me how to reframe my thoughts and approach problems with more constructive solutions. The focus of TSP is on developing thinking skills directly related to offending behaviours, such as emotional awareness, problem-solving, and recognising risk factors. These sessions encouraged me to reflect deeply on the decisions and thought patterns that contributed to my re-offending, helping me recognise how I could have handled certain situations better.

Initially, I found the sessions difficult, especially the role-playing exercises, and I would often refuse to participate. Being in a predominantly male group added to my discomfort; apart from one female facilitator, I was the only woman in the sessions. This made it hard to open up, as I often felt out of place and vulnerable. However, as my confidence and self-esteem began to grow, I became more engaged with the group, gradually feeling comfortable enough to contribute actively.

AA Fellowship: A Journey of Belonging and Healing

I'm not sure there is a God, but I do believe there is a higher power - I'm just not entirely sure what it is. This uncertainty didn't stop me from finding immense support through the Alcoholics Anonymous (AA) fellowship. Attending AA meetings became one of the most powerful steps in my recovery journey. In those meetings, I found a sense of belonging and understanding that I hadn't found anywhere else. Being in the presence of people who truly "*got it*" - individuals who had lived through similar struggles with addiction, trauma, and despair - was transformative. Sharing my story with others who understood the depths of my pain made me feel less isolated. Hearing their experiences reminded me that I was not alone in this battle.

One of the most valuable aspects of AA was the opportunity to attend women-only meetings. These groups provided a space where I could speak freely about the unique struggles women face in recovery - particularly the trauma, emotional burdens, and societal pressures that are often compounded for women in addiction. In these women-only groups, I could open up about things I wouldn't have felt comfortable discussing in a larger, mixed-gender setting. The ability to connect with other women who had faced similar battles helped me feel seen, heard, and understood in ways that were sometimes difficult to achieve elsewhere. This sense of solidarity became crucial to my healing, helping me build a supportive network of women who truly understood my journey.

The most crucial part of AA was learning to forgive myself. For so long, I had carried the weight of regret and shame. The decisions I had made, the harm I had caused others, and the mistakes of my past haunted me, making it difficult to move forward. But through the support I received from therapy, AA, and the women I connected with in the fellowship, I began to realise that I wasn't defined by my past mistakes. Recovery, for me, became about healing the wounds within - letting go of the shame and guilt I had carried for so long. With the help of the programme and my new network of support, I learned to accept myself.

Conclusion: The Unique Pathways of Women in the Criminal Justice System

As I reflect on my recovery journey, it's clear to me that the path for women in the drug recovery and the criminal justice system is vastly different from that of men. For women like me, the journey is often shaped by a combination of factors that are unique to our experiences - factors such as trauma, abuse, and societal expectations about women. We face emotional and psychological struggles that are often overlooked or misunderstood by a system that tends to be designed with men in mind. Women often carry the additional weight of caregiving responsibilities, the stigmas surrounding motherhood, and societal pressures to conform to roles that don't always serve our healing. For many of us, the need to nurture and the lack of support can be incredibly isolating, making recovery even more challenging.

Now, as I continue my recovery journey, I recognise that support is not a weakness - it is a strength. For so long, I tried to face my struggles alone, believing that asking for help made me weak. But recovery has taught me that healing is not something we do alone. It takes community, compassion, and a willingness to face the pain to rise stronger. The AA fellowship, therapy, and other supportive relationships have been central to my healing process.

Five years ago, I would never have imagined reaching this point. I've grown into someone who is not only willing to share my story but also confident in the value of my voice. I've spoken in Parliament and recently presented at a prison reform conference. I have also taken part in podcasts, blogs, media interviews, and presented at a webinar of 100 magistrates and much more.

Sharing my journey with others, especially those who may be in positions of power, has been an empowering experience. It was a moment of showing how far I've come, from a place of shame and isolation to a position of strength and purpose. What once terrified me - talking on camera, in front of people, or expressing my thoughts - has become a skill I am steadily developing, despite years of feeling criticised and judged by those around me.

I believe these changes have happened because I've altered my behaviour toward others, no longer blaming them for my past mistakes. It hasn't been easy, but I've had to own up to my wrongs and accept them to move forward. It's a process of forgiveness, not just toward others, but also toward myself. I do have to remind myself to be kind to myself, acknowledging that I am not a failure and that focusing on the future is more important than dwelling on past mistakes.

I am now building relationships with my children - something I never had before and that feels like another significant piece of my life finally coming together. For women in recovery, rebuilding relationships, particularly with children, can be one of the most powerful aspects of healing. The process of learning to be the mother I always wanted to be has been both difficult and rewarding, but it has shown me the value of resilience and forgiveness in ways I couldn't have imagined earlier in my journey.

I learned to acknowledge my past without allowing it to control me. It is a long and difficult journey, but with each small step forward, I began to rebuild my sense of self-worth and hope for the future. For women, recovery is not just about escaping addiction or crime - it's about reclaiming our identities, building new relationships, and finally healing from the traumas that shaped our paths. Our journeys are unique, often more complex and multifaceted than those of men, but with the right support, compassion, and determination, recovery is possible. Our voices, our stories, and our resilience have the power to inspire change - not only in our own lives but in the drug treatment, recovery and criminal justice system itself.

The Future Looks Bright

Lena Verve

Today I believe in tomorrow, I accept where I am and where I have been, and that what I do today decides my future, it is in my hands and only mine. I no longer dwell on the past, on the shame or guilt, I use it as the strength to push me forwards and to build a future that doesn't scare me. Those feelings, which once consumed me and prevented me seeking help, have been replaced with a sense of pride, respect and compassion for myself that I hadn't thought was possible. The determination and resilience it took to overcome these barriers has provided me with an ability to use my experience to help others do the same, through working in recovery services, and for this I feel humbled and privileged.

It's a stark contrast to two years ago, when I felt trapped in the chaos I'd created, I couldn't see a way out, playing with fire when it came to my life. I had lost all control and had given up so much that once brought meaning to my existence; friends and partners I loved, a career that provided me with purpose, and a sense of who I truly was. I despised the hollow shell of a person I had become, and I was ready to surrender to my addiction, I had given up on living.

While the life I have today isn't what I would have envisioned for myself, I'm not sure I'd change it. The lessons I've learned, the people I've encountered, and the profound impact of their stories and friendships have shaped me into the person I am today, someone strong, kind, and compassionate. I am deeply grateful for this second chance at life and the confidence my recovery has finally allowed me to discover after so long struggling to accept myself.

My Journey with Alcohol

I had a stable upbringing and a strong circle of friends; I had never experienced or witnessed domestic or sexual abuse. I seemed to have the world at my feet, yet something always pulled me towards alcohol from the very first time I tried it, I loved it. It gave me a sense of confidence that I had lost during the awkwardness of adolescence, and I could only regain that confidence through drinking. I enjoyed how it made me feel "*fun*" and the attention I received from boys. However, as depression began to set in during my early twenties, I became drawn to it even more for the escape it provided from my difficult emotions, low self-esteem, and the constant berating of myself.

The first time I turned to destructive behaviours for comfort was in my early twenties, following a relationship breakdown, when I developed an eating disorder. It began with comfort eating, which quickly escalated into binging and purging. Eventually, I found myself overeating and binge eating without purging, leading to a gradual loss of control over my eating habits. As my weight began to creep up, my self-esteem plummeted. Ashamed of my coping mechanisms, I often hid my eating and began isolating myself, reluctant to socialise with others as my confidence waned. I couldn't bear the thought of people looking at me. In my early twenties, appearance felt so important, and I felt immense pressure to meet certain standards. As people started making comments about my weight gain, I withdrew further and turned to food for solace. This self-imposed isolation and the need to conceal what I viewed as a disgusting and shameful habit mirrored my struggles with alcoholism, with alcohol eventually replacing food as my escape.

With the drink, my weight would fluctuate depending on whether I could keep food down as well as the drink or if I had an appetite. So I went from podgy and bloated to being underweight with a beer belly towards the end, when I couldn't manage food.

My skin was dry and flaky, my lips were cracked and chipped, my face was puffy and swollen, always covered in bruises, one black eye would heal only to be replaced by another. I looked ghostly pale, almost grey, as if life was slowly draining out of me.

Driven by a need to find comfort, these behaviours spiralled out of control, becoming increasingly destructive and giving me even more reason to turn to self-medication until I reached a point where I could no longer function. I felt utterly repulsive, like I was rotting from the inside out and consumed by self-hatred. I remember staring at myself in the mirror of the bathroom in the hospital. I hadn't looked in the mirror for weeks and I didn't recognise what stared back at me, I felt completely detached and broken.

This admission to hospital was not long after I was told that if I carried on the way I was with my drinking, I would only last another six months. My mum had started to tell my siblings to prepare themselves for the inevitable. By this point I had accepted that my addiction was going to kill me. The last few years of my drinking had seen me on a rapid downwards spiral. There had been many times where my mental health, my outlook and self esteem had been so low that I contemplated killing myself several times a day, I'd be at the station on the way to work and fantasise about jumping in front of the train, and of the relief everyone would get from it finally being over, but I never had the guts to go through with it. In my eyes that was just another example of me failing at something, which added to the existing disgust I felt in myself.

It was the final few months of my drinking that I felt a shift, I could feel my body shutting down, it felt different in a way I still can't explain. The pure effort and pain to do the simplest of tasks was exhausting. The symptoms of my withdrawal would start as soon as I woke up and only increase in severity the longer I tried to resist having that fateful first drink. These effects would range from sweating, shivering and skin crawling to shaking so much I couldn't even walk to the bathroom unaided, usually to vomit bile. Insomnia due to heightened anxiety and a racing heart meant that I couldn't sleep to get any relief, and even when I did I would soon be woken by convulsions, hallucinations and nightmares.

The combination of feeling my body give up and mentally giving up meant I finally felt ready to let go and die. It seemed too hard and impossible to ever recover. I felt I'd gone too far and there was no way back. My mum had become my carer, trying to get me to eat, monitoring my drink which had now become medicine to me. I wouldn't wash because I feared having another seizure in the shower. I couldn't hold myself up anyway or bear to catch my reflection in the mirror. My hair had become matted, and my mum had to try and brush through it for me, some bits were so bad I just cut it out with the kitchen scissors. I had reverted to being a helpless child again and I could see the worry etched all over my mum's face. I hated myself and felt like a worthless waste of space and I knew without doubt my family would be better off without me. I just hoped the end would come sooner rather than later, for one day to not wake up and finally be released from it all. I no longer left the house, day after day, trapped in the endless cycle of drinking and withdrawal, it was relentless. I would dread waking up in a bed wet with sweat or even soiled, covered in fresh bruises and black eyes that I had no recollection of getting and the cravings and withdrawal hitting me as soon as I came round, I just wanted it all to end.

My Last Drink

And it did, on the 16th November 2022, I had what I hope will be my last drink. It had finally got to 4pm which was the time I had to wait until my first drink. I could finally relieve some of the withdrawal but as I had experienced a few years earlier, I felt my vision go, the intense shaking, the panic growing, and I could tell I was about to have a seizure. I managed to get my dad, and he called an ambulance. The last thing I remembered before I lay down to let it happen was him telling the phone handler that his daughter was an alcoholic and was having a seizure. Even at this point, I still felt immense shame at being referred to as an alcoholic. I closed my eyes and thought that finally this was it.

After being taken to hospital by ambulance I suffered another severe seizure. Due to the bruising on my face from previous falls, I was rushed into a CT scan as they thought I may have a bleed on the brain. I only know this as a day or so later I asked my dad why my tongue was so badly blistered and he told me I'd bit my tongue badly in the second seizure, which I had no memory of. I only remembered still uncontrollably shaking as I was being put into the capsule for my scan and being asked to stay still and failing. What followed was a five-day stay in hospital, where I was emergency detoxed and went into psychosis from the withdrawal. I genuinely believed I had been kidnapped and was being kept in a crack den. I kept calling the police and trying to escape, resulting in two security guards being put on the doors of the ward to try and keep me under control.

Everything Felt New Again

The days, weeks, and months following my initial release from the hospital were a bit of a blur. I felt incredibly fragile and still in shock over how close I had come to losing my life, and I was determined not to go back there. Everything felt fresh and new, I knew that this was it; I had been given a second chance. While I may well have another drink in me, I knew I didn't have another recovery in me. Some refer to it as a spiritual awakening, but something undeniably shifted within me. I found the resolve to fight for my life once more. I embraced who I was and recognised what needed to be done, I wanted to rebuild my life and restore my relationships.

In the rooms of AA and the support groups at the local drug and alcohol service, I often found myself staring at the walls. I would observe the people around me and listen to their stories of trauma and addiction. The atmosphere was thick with sadness, despair, and desperation, and I'd think, "*How the hell did it come to this*?" Yet, I only let that thought pass through my mind; it didn't matter how I had arrived at this point. All that mattered was that I accepted my situation, and in that moment, I realised there was nowhere else in the world I needed to be if I wanted to get better.

Over the following months, I started going to a 12-step program. I gradually rebuilt my self-esteem and was finally able to look in the mirror again. I started repairing my relationships with myself, my family, and my friends. I made an effort to be a good daughter, sister, aunt, and friend, all the roles I had neglected for so long, and I worked to restore the broken trust. However, two roles I had once desperately wanted in my life were not there to be repaired; I was no one's wife or girlfriend, nor was I anyone's mother.

Not Conforming to Society's Expectations

My romantic relationships had all been collateral damage during my active addiction. No relationship had been more important than the one I had with the bottle. Although I am grateful that I didn't have any children as they would have without doubt been taken from my care, the role of a mother is one I have been coming to accept may never be mine. Not only is it a question of whether or not nature would allow it, it would also feel to me like too much of a risk, to myself and to any child I might have. That is something that plays on my mind a lot, it's something that I seldom hear discussed either. I hear many stories from women about the children they had removed, but rarely do I hear from the would-be mothers who, because of addiction, have that dream of motherhood removed.

I also carried immense guilt and shame from a teenage pregnancy, which ended in a late term abortion. At age 17 I found this traumatic, especially as after spending the day in hospital with nothing happening, I was sent home. Once home I had a tiny but what appeared to be a fully formed foetus on the toilet, hanging down between my legs from its umbilical cord. The placenta still inside me, that I had to pull out. I laid it on the side of the bathroom for a while, staring at what I had created and then destroyed. Then I wrapped it in toilet paper and put it in a pot to take back to the hospital the next day. I slept with the pot next to me. Like my drinking, I ignored the pregnancy for as long as I could, hoping it would just go away, as the decision I made wasn't one I wanted to make. I always felt that I would be punished for that choice, it weighed heavy on my mind and I often felt that maybe my addiction and the impact it had on my prospect of motherhood was deserved.

So, in my sobriety, I had to adjust to what I believed the future would hold. I no longer envisioned having my own family due to fear and also I was for the first time getting to know myself properly. The two main roles society expects of every woman, being a wife and a mother, may not be what I truly want or what would give me my second chance at life, or the purpose I desired. My feelings around motherhood remain ambiguous, whilst I have great joy in seeing my friends and sister become amazing mothers, I would be lying if I didn't sometimes find it bittersweet and feel pangs of sadness about the uncertainty I feel around motherhood. For now, I will just focus on renewed love and appreciation for life and see how my future unfolds. If motherhood isn't to be, or I decide it's not for me, I know I will still have a full and happy life beyond what I thought was ever possible in my darkest days.

Healing and Nurturing Existing Relationships

My love for my family allowed me to build the strength I needed to recover, and I have no doubt that without their love and support I would be dead. Today I focus on nurturing the relationships that withstood the strain I put them under. I try to be better for all the people that I love so much but neglected for years, to thank them for sticking by me when I made it so difficult to do so.

My relationship with my mother needed the most work. After years of looking after us I took her straight back to caring for me as though I was a child again. I said and did hurtful and spiteful things, she would often do the same in retaliation. We were never a family who was good with emotions and feelings. I also had to consider that this may have been something which contributed to me turning to alcohol for comfort. I was an overly sensitive and anxious person from a young age. I hadn't always felt able to turn to my family for the comfort I needed. I felt intrinsically that I was very different from them for being too emotional, and it was often a very lonely place to be.

This wasn't me trying to place blame on anyone. Recovery from addiction is about taking accountability and I owned my wrong doings. Accepting my family relationships might have been a factor that was very difficult for me to contemplate, but if I was to move forward with healthy coping mechanisms I had to identify where uncomfortable feelings might have stemmed from. I needed to feel comfortable saying when I needed assurance from loved ones to prevent me from falling into old habits. My family have done that, they are incredibly kind and patient when I need it. I feel that this ability to be more open about my feelings has strengthened all my relationships.

This strengthened bond was incredibly important when my dad died unexpectedly after a short illness earlier this year. My dad was someone I loved and trusted deeply, the person I felt most safe with. I always felt his unconditional love and support without it being said. I knew he would do anything for me, but I could never bring myself to talk to him in any detail about what was going on and how I felt. I know that this made him feel helpless, maybe even isolated or rejected by me. I could snap at him and be irritable with him in a way that I wouldn't dare with my mum. I still don't understand why I wasn't able to open up to him, and one of the things that pained me most when he died was that he might have died not knowing how much I loved him. He deserved to know how much I adored him, but I struggled to express it. I hope wherever he is that he is now, he is in no doubt that he, my mum and siblings are the loves of my life and he forever holds the most precious place in my heart. I feel so lucky to have been his daughter.

Perhaps the reason I couldn't talk about it was because I still wanted to be his little girl. I didn't want to talk about how much I felt I'd let him down and disappointed him through my addiction. One thing I was incredibly grateful for was that he saw me get well before he died. I am also grateful that my recovery gave me the strength and the tools to be able to cope with his death without relapsing. I was able to be present and support my family, rather than become an additional burden, I owed them that and so much more. I genuinely believe you can't get sober for anyone but yourself, but you can stay sober for others and having that love for my family keeps me sober.

Getting to Know Myself Again

I have fought hard for the person I am now and could be, and for the people that I loved who I began to realise must dearly love me too. My relationship with myself is one which is very much a work in progress, even two years on it is something I can often struggle with. That low self esteem, the level of utter contempt for myself, my feelings of worthlessness and a kind of inferiority that at points so severe I didn't think I deserved a space on this earth ran deep. I had completely lost myself in addiction and I had no idea who I was anymore. I was once quite naturally cheerful, positive, and caring but I became crippled with anxiety, anger, sadness, became manipulative and self-pitying.

Through support groups and 12-steps, I got to know myself again without my emotional support crutch. I became less selfish, I tried to be a better person to the people around me. I was caring, patient and considerate to the other people in my recovery. I listened to their stories and felt genuine empathy for them. I grew in confidence as I grew stronger. I kept going, day by day when it would have been so much easier to give in and slowly I began to acknowledge the amazing courage and resilience this took. I started to like myself again, I was kind to myself, I was proud even and I started to recognise myself again.

People say that when you get into sobriety you go back to the age when your addiction started. I had been an addict at one level or another for all of my twenties and I had no idea who I was anymore. I was forced to spend time with myself, reflect and try and understand who I was and who I wanted to be. I became kinder, more empathetic, thoughtful and resilient in all aspects of my life.

Sober dating was a daunting prospect, I always craved the attention and admiration from the opposite sex in my drinking days but now I wanted to be loved and cared for. I had never been on a date sober and had no idea how to do it, but I surprised myself with the amount of confidence I approached dating. I finally accepted who I was and had a level of respect for myself that I had never experienced before. Sober dating remains a part of my life, but I've also discovered that my happiness and my worth is not defined by a relationship with a man. I am the only person in control of that and I won't settle for someone who threatens to disrupt the peace I've found within myself. Finding the right person remains a work in progress, but not something which holds a priority in my life the way it once did. Previously I saw someone being my boyfriend as some sort of validation that I was lovable or valuable. So the horrors of sober dating persist, but it certainly provides some entertainment.

Pressure From the Media

I had grown up in the 90's and early noughties and I was inspired by girl power from the Spice Girls and ladette culture of the time, showing girls could give men a run for their money in all aspects of life, even football as seen in "*Bend it like Beckham.*" Girls and women were encouraged to be a mix of the best of both genders. We were told we could "*have it all*" which is of course empowering, but it comes with its own very real pressures. Men only had one role, women now had to juggle careers, children, maintaining a home and whilst also remaining attractive to the opposite sex. The women in shows like Sex and the City when I was a teenager were my role models, successful, beautiful and always of course, with a cocktail in hand. Society and the media glamourise drinking and tells you that you need a drink to have fun, you're told you're boring if you don't have a drink. I know I always felt more "*fun*" with half a litre of Lambrini down me, because, you know; "*Lambrini girls just wanna have fun*" but as soon as it becomes a problem for someone, no one wants to know. We have a very hypocritical culture when it comes to drinking and these double standards create stereotypes which are as deadly as the substance itself.

I Didn't Fit the Stereotype

The stereotype I had in my head of an alcoholic as a smelly, homeless old man on a park bench, who had probably been traumatised by a life of neglect and abuse, created a self stigma that prevented me from getting help any earlier, and almost cost me my life. The strong desire to not be associated with what I saw as weakness, dirty, unattractive and certainly unfeminine, created an additional barrier on top of the existing ones created from societal stigma. In addition to this, I felt unworthy of help because I hadn't experienced any of the trauma that leads people to self medicate in the destructive way that I was. What right did I have to ruin my life when there are so many people that would have killed to have even a fraction of my fortune? This also seemed to be the attitude of many of the people when I made tentative steps towards help. I quite often felt I wasn't taken seriously when I tried to explain the extent of my problems, and to get to the point where I had built the courage to ask for help to then be dismissed, only reinforced two things that I felt. One, that maybe it wasn't as bad as I thought it was, and so was I being dramatic. Secondly, that I was wasting people's time which should be reserved for those who actually deserved help.

The emphasis on looks and appearance was one of the things that prevented me even acknowledging I had a problem, before it prevented me seeking help. It always perplexed me why I ended up an addict, but I don't fit the stereotype of an alcoholic. I'm a white, young, attractive middle-class woman who never wanted for anything my entire life. I am also acutely aware that these privileges are also the reason I was able to recover and have managed to remain abstinent.

Additionally, some people tried to protect me from what they perceived to be an environment that would be too difficult for me. The probation officer I had to report to after I was convicted for drink driving cried when she met me. I was classed as a high-risk offender for blowing four times the limit. I'd had to cancel my first appointment with her because I had been hospitalised after having a seizure following the two-week bender I went on after being arrested. I wasn't what she expected. She said I reminded her of her daughter who was a similar age and struggling with loneliness. She felt that it could just have easily been her daughter sitting there and she would get emotional when I talked about what had happened and how I was feeling. She looked at me and said *"Lily, what do you see when you look in the mirror? You're beautiful."* I was very confused by her reaction to me and she became very maternal towards me which although came from a good place, created its own barriers. I had been told by the hospital to self refer myself to NECA which was the drug and alcohol service in the town and she advised me not to because she thought I would be vulnerable around the other people accessing the service. Although it was her way of trying to protect me, what she didn't realise was that she was reinforcing a belief that I didn't belong there, simply because I didn't look the part.

She wasn't wrong, when I attended the court ordered drink driving course every Tuesday night, I was the only female present out of 12 people. I was also the youngest person there by about 10 years which was intimidating at times. Being in the high-risk category meant that many of us had drinking problems and often turned up drunk to the session. One man took a shine to me and made inappropriate comments to me which got him in trouble with his probation officer, forcing him to apologise to me, which just made me more uncomfortable.

The truth is I am no different from anyone else who needs help with addiction. We are all just very ill, broken people. Addiction doesn't discriminate, it doesn't care who you are and once it has a hold on you, we're all fair game.

Male Dominated Recovery Spaces

Later when I did end up accessing drug and alcohol services, most support groups were male dominated, and I often felt dismissed by them. In one group, we had gone round and talked a bit about ourselves, I had explained my seizures, psychosis and delirium tremors from withdrawal, losing jobs, and partners. During the break, me and one man were the only ones left inside as we didn't smoke, and he turned and said *"so what are you doing here again anyway? Drank a few too many glasses of wine, ended up in hospital getting your stomach pumped so mummy and daddy sent you here?"*

I brushed his comments off and said *"something like that"* just so that he would leave me alone. But it felt as if there was some sort of hierarchy in addiction. I didn't fit the criteria to deserve help, and I felt belittled. At least by this point, although it sometimes intimidated me, I knew I was exactly where I needed to be. At an earlier stage I would have seen this as the validation I needed to tell me that I was in the wrong place, further preventing me from getting the help I desperately needed.

The Power of the Recovery Community

Thankfully, I knew I was exactly where I needed to be and I just kept going back to groups as they had told me to. I started attending AA meetings as well, where the shares of other women inspired and empowered me. I was humbled and blown away by people's kindness which I felt unworthy of. As the weeks and months rolled on, recovery groups and communities taught me that I am deserving of kindness, that I am not a bad person, I am not a weak person. I might have said and done bad things but I was allowed to forgive myself and seek forgiveness from others. It taught me how to use my experience to help others, how to feel and express gratitude, how to take accountability for my past, live in the day and by doing so, take control of my own future. I have a confidence in myself that I wouldn't have without recovery, a genuine belief that I can do whatever I set my mind to, because I have proved to myself that I can achieve things which I deemed impossible.

The Power of Friendship with Other Women

The relationships I've created with other women in particular have created a sense of community and given me a sense of belonging that I hadn't felt before. I could belly laugh with these women at some of the lighter stories, the chaos and absurdity of it all, something anyone in recovery will tell you is only possible to do with those who have walked the same path as you. I feel strong and empowered when I'm with these women, who are now my friends for life, and there is a deep level of understanding and acceptance between us that is difficult to articulate and feels unbreakable. I know I can be completely open with them, unashamedly my authentic self, and trust them to have only my best interests at heart, which after years of feeling ashamed of who I am, is incredibly comforting and reassuring. These women are from all walks of life, different ages, different stories and their incredible journeys have brought us together, a shared experience few who have not lived through it can understand. I value each and everyone of those relationships as one of the best things to come from addiction.

A Life of Possibilities

Recovery feels to me like my superpower, I have recovered from an all-consuming addiction which most people lose their battle with. I have proved to myself that I can do the hard things, things which seemed impossible or out of reach, I know that if I put my mind to something I can achieve it. Before my addiction took hold, I used to love running and I slowly began to run again once I had my strength back and I gave myself the goal of completing a marathon by the end of the year. I saw it as a metaphor for my recovery, if I could recover from addiction, I could run a marathon. I just kept putting one foot in front of the other, I proved to myself that the pain passes, nothing lasts forever, just keep going and you'll make it. So I went from being unable to walk up the stairs to running a marathon in less than a year. This achievement represented so much more to me than 26.2 miles, it was my journey from the depths of despair to a life full of possibilities.

My journey in recovery has been impacted by being a woman in different ways, from the societal burdens of what a woman should be, the double standards in what is expected from us. The stereotypes of what it is to be an alcoholic, what it looks like and who that makes you, which stands in the way of accepting you have a problem and seeking help. Male dominated and misogynistic spaces in recovery which are intimidating and isolating, reinforcing preconceived notions. Undoubtedly women face many barriers in addiction and recovery, but the empowerment and self-worth that is gained from the bonds with other women in recovery is powerful and unparalleled. The feelings of acceptance and belonging which has given me the confidence to find and use my voice again, the comfort that this acceptance has provided me, so that I no longer seek external validation has helped me put the pieces of my life back together.

My journey through recovery has been shaped in unique ways by my experience as a woman. From the weight of societal expectations telling us who we should be, to the frustrating double standards that define what's expected of us, these challenges have often felt overwhelming. The stereotypes around addiction, what an alcoholic is "*supposed*" to look like and what that means for your identity create barriers that make it difficult to recognise when help is needed and even harder to ask for it. Male-dominated, often misogynistic spaces in recovery can feel isolating and intimidating, reinforcing outdated beliefs that it's not a space for women.

But despite these barriers, the strength and resilience I've found through connecting with other women in recovery have been transformative. There's an incredible power in the bonds we build, an unspoken understanding, a shared journey of healing, and an unwavering support that gives life back its meaning. The sense of acceptance and belonging I've experienced has helped me reclaim my voice and shown me the value of seeking validation from within. With each step forward, I've been able to piece my broken life back together into something I'm proud of, no longer hiding in shame, I have an appreciation of the journey that I've been on so that I never take one day for granted. There is nothing stronger than a broken woman who has rebuilt her life.

Life Began at 40

Claire Naughton

My name is Claire and I am an alcoholic, I've been in recovery from alcohol dependency since September 2013. I work as the National Coordinator for Recovery Academy Ireland and have been in post since November 2022. The Recovery Academy was set up in Ireland initially to promote and champion the concept of recovery. I have been involved with the Academy since the beginning having signed up as a member initially. Never in a million years did I think back then that I would be in the position I'm in now. Before I started working for the Academy, I worked in homeless services in Dublin specifically designed to support women who had completed residential treatment for addiction issues. I am in the second year of studying a Masters in Addiction Recovery in Trinity College Dublin whilst working full time and I am 51 years old.

I live alone very close to the beach in North County Dublin and my life is pretty full between work, college, family and friends. My home is my haven and I am so grateful for it. I am currently in a fairly new long-distance romantic relationship which to be perfectly honest, suits me down to the ground. I have no expectations about where it will go but I know I am enjoying the journey. My mum and sister live about an hour's drive away in County Westmeath, I have a really good relationship with my mum and this has always been the case, she has been my biggest supporter. My sister Marie lives next door to my mum with her family so I try to get down to visit as often as I can. I lost my other sister Michelle two years ago to addiction, she passed away on her own in a stranger's flat. We are still waiting for the inquest to see exactly what happened. My brother Peter lives in Belfast with his wife, I don't really see them much. I have a few close female friends whom I could ring in the middle of the night and know they would answer the phone if I needed them. Like my family, my friendships are extremely important to me. My friends are the people who I can tell absolutely anything to without fear of judgement or rejection. Although I am quite maternal, I don't have any children of my own. Addiction took hold of me in my thirties and the thought of starting a family didn't even enter my head. This is something I have reflected on over the last few years, probably because I am menopausal and any chance I may have had has passed now. I have three nieces and seven nephews, and I am close with most of them and see them as the children I never had. I do have a niece I haven't seen since she was a baby, my brother's daughter. Her mum cut all contact with our whole family when she split from my brother, I hope one day we can meet and maybe start to get to know her. One of my nephews is in the care of the state due to my sister Michelle's alcoholism, he is nearly 15 and has been in care since birth. I tried to get access to him when I was two years sober but was blocked every step of the way by the social workers. Since Michelle passed away I have been seeing my nephew regularly, he is in the care of a wonderful woman and her family. I often reflect on the times I tried before to see my nephew, the social work department are more than happy for me to be involved now but it took a long time to get here and a lot of years were wasted.

My mental health these days is fairly good, although I have had quite low periods particularly when I started experiencing perimenopause symptoms just after I had turned 48. I didn't have a clue what was going on with me, I was drug and alcohol free but my mind went what I can only describe as "*very dark*". I felt similar to how I felt towards the end of my active addiction days. I didn't care whether I lived or died and although there were no plans to drink or use, I was concerned at the time that I was in relapse mode. A trip to the doctor told me exactly what was going on, I was perimenopausal and the doctor assured me that everything I had been saying made perfect sense, my oestrogen levels were practically non-existent. I was put on a small dose of HRT and could honestly feel the benefits within a week. These days I do a small bit of yoga and walking to keep active but I'm no gym bunny! It's just not my thing. I am in a Fellowship and feel very grateful to have found my people. I love my life today. There is no one I would rather be today, a long shot from the person I was before I came into Recovery. Life is good and I very much keep it in the day.

Recovery has given me a second chance at life literally. Today as busy as my life is I try to keep it as simple as I possibly can. I have to prioritise my mental health above everything else because I know where it has brought me to before. I actually love myself today, not in an egotistical way but in a way I never had before. I always put others needs before my own and would do anything just to keep the peace and hope you'd like me. I actually don't care today, that's what Recovery has given me, freedom to be me and to know I am good enough.

The Party Drug Scene

My addiction issues definitely started during my teens in Manchester where I am originally from. I started to mess with recreational drugs. I was 19 years old, the Hacienda nightclub was the place to be at the time and acid house music was huge in Manchester. I tried acid, ecstasy and weed but my favourite was speed. I absolutely loved it so much so that if I couldn't get it I couldn't see the point in going out.

I started studying nursing in October 1992 where I moved from the family home to Preston. It soon became clear the partying was more of a priority to me than my studies and for this reason and the fact my mum and step dad sold the family home to move to Ireland in 1993, I decided to quit nursing after a year. I told myself it was the right thing to do as I had two younger sisters who were in Manchester and I always saw myself as a bit of a caretaker, having a father who walked out when I was four years old and starting a new family probably contributed to this. I always felt I had to take on responsibility to help my mum. The reality now when I look back was, I couldn't keep up with my studies and I was more interested in going out and having fun!

I was working in a nursing home as a care assistant back in Manchester, living with my sisters and had fallen for a lad who I was absolutely besotted with, he also happened to be a bit of a ladies man and a dealer. Andy, he was my first love. The only problem was I wasn't his. I pined after Andy for over a year taking the breadcrumbs of time and affection that he offered gladly and slowly but surely, I found myself drinking and using during the week. I knew the speed taking was getting out of control when I was using going into work so I knew I needed to do something. Things were getting worse with Andy and deep down I knew it wasn't going to work and that I was hurting myself more and more by staying in the situation.

Starting a New Life

In April 1994 I decided to leave the job and go to Ireland on an extended holiday to give myself a break from the speed and try to get my thoughts together. I never saw my drinking as being a problem. I come from a large Mancunian/Irish family and alcohol was involved in every part of that. Once I was there I decided to stay in Ireland! I got myself a little job in a restaurant as a waitress and started my new life. It didn't bother me about the drugs side of things because it wasn't available in the town in Ireland where I was living and I was happy enough going out Friday, Saturday and Sunday all day drinking.

For the next ten years I carried on working and partying, my motto was work hard, party harder. I'd left the restaurant and got work in a factory. I liked factory work, clocking in and out with no responsibilities. Problem was, I am a grafter and I'd always excelled in any jobs I had been in. Starting as a general operator and working my way up to a senior management position in the company. I wasn't really interested in meeting anyone to settle down with. There were brief relationships and situationships but nothing serious. My drinking hadn't been causing any major issues in my life except for the odd works night out when I'd insult my boss and have absolutely no memory of it or get into a fight with someone when out with my friends.

I'll never forget the day my mobile phone rang in 2005 and the voice on the other end although it sounded familiar, I couldn't for the life of me figure out who it was. "*Hiya, it's me Andy*", I replied "*Andy who*" and then the penny dropped. It was my Andy. I felt like I was 19 again, (I was actually 33 at this point) all the feelings came rushing back and once again I was smitten. I had bought my own house by this time and had what looked on the outside like I had my shit together. I had a good job, I owned my own house and I had a decent car. The truth is on the inside I was insecure and had serious low self-esteem issues. Reconnecting with Andy brought all of this to the fore and I found myself more and more relying on alcohol. I'd say the initial six months after he got back in touch with me, my drinking went to another level. I had to have a bottle of wine just to have a conversation with him on the phone some days. I knew after this time that he hadn't changed. We stayed friends but my drinking escalated.

Things Were Falling Apart

I quit my job in 2007 because at this stage I couldn't perform in my role. I was going into work shaking so badly because my body needed alcohol to stop the shakes at this point. I couldn't pay the mortgage so I lost my house and ended up moving back to my mums for a short while before moving back to Manchester in October 2007. That December my step dad had a massive heart attack and died suddenly. I returned to Ireland to live with my mum. I stayed for 6 months before going back to Manchester and moving in with my childhood best friend. After six weeks she gave me an ultimatum, either I go to AA or I had to leave her home. I did as she asked and lasted 6 weeks before picking up a drink. I moved out of her home and in with my cousin. Daily drinking was the norm for so long. I needed it to function so I would sit in the bedroom with the curtains closed and drink around the clock.

Things deteriorated between my cousin and me due to my drinking and I ended up moving in with someone I had worked with briefly who drank like I did. Mark was a cocaine addict and an alcoholic. He was also prone to giving me a good beating quite regularly. It was fairly normal to see me with a black eye or covered in bruises. I distanced myself from my family, in some way protecting him and my drinking escalated. Mark didn't question my drinking; he was my supplier. He would allocate me drink and cigarettes and I was totally dependent on him. He was an insurance broker so his work was on the phone. I did a lot of admin work for him and cold calling to secure him deals. He paid me in drink and smokes and put a roof over my head. I could drink without anyone questioning me and giving me grief about it. I didn't see it at the time, but he totally controlled my every movement.

I would still meet up with Andy who lived very close to where I was living whenever I could. One day after Mark had locked me in his office for 12 hours without water, food, alcohol or smokes he gave me the beating of all beatings. After a couple of days my face was black on one side and I walked into a pub where Andy drank. He wasn't there but his friend was. His friend asked what had happened, I obviously made something up but he took a photo of my face and sent it to Andy. Andy went ballistic, threatening to do all sorts to Mark. I did go back to Mark's that evening and told him Andy knew. I got another good hiding but this time he stayed away from my face. The next day I got a call off my sister to say Andy had been killed in a hit and run the night before. I later learned he had been to see a friend of Marks to find out where he lived. Andy died instantly. I was completely devastated and drank solid for 2 weeks before I could sense Mark was on the verge of hitting me again. This time I knew I had to get out. I returned to Ireland in 2010 with the help of my mum who was worried sick and I stayed with her. Drinking daily and not knowing how to stop, or not being able to stop. In 2012, I was offered a job in Wales with my old boss from the factory. I moved to Wales thinking this would fix me. All I needed was a change of environment. How wrong I was. At this point I was going into work under the influence and it wasn't long before I was sacked. Another return to Ireland. My sister had to actually fly over to collect my car because I was constantly under the influence.

I Was Going to Die

I tried to stop drinking with the help of my doctor but nothing could stop me. I had some dry spells where I thought I mustn't be an alcoholic because of the brief dry periods. These dry periods were always followed by drinking sprees that lasted for months. Eventually after not showering for a at least a week I was brought back to the doctor in my pyjamas. I had just turned 40 a week before. Although I was constantly drunk and unable to remember anything I remember this next bit very clearly. My doctor took his glasses off his head and threw them on his desk and said "*I can't do anymore for you, you're going to die*". I could see the frustration and complete despair in his face. He asked if I would go into treatment to which I replied "*yes*". I have since spoken to the doctor and reminded him of his words to me that day. He apologised and said he shouldn't have spoken to me in that way and could be struck off for doing so. I've thanked him numerous times and told him that was exactly what I needed to hear because that was the start of my recovery journey. Something shifted inside me that day when he said those words to me. I had known I was dying but to hear him say it was another thing. I left the surgery that day and bought alcohol, it was a Friday. I was in a treatment centre in Cork by Monday morning. I specifically wanted to go to an all-female centre as I knew men could be a distraction for me. I had seen my sister go into treatment centres and come out with a partner and pregnant very soon after. I didn't want that. If I was going to do this, I was going to give it my all.

I stayed in treatment for 11 weeks and 3 days. It should have been 12 weeks but my sister arrived into detox so they shipped me out as fast as they could. I was one of the lucky ones who secured a bed in a transition house in Dublin city. I stayed there for 8 months. I lived with other women who were in early recovery and one of the conditions was that I had to go to an AA meeting every day. Sometimes I hated it but on a deep level I knew I needed it. This was fine whilst I was in the house but once I left the transition house and moved into a women's homeless accommodation there was nobody telling me I had to get a meeting. I was left to my own devices. There were some really tough times in that period, I was trying to do it my way, I thought not drinking would be enough. I soon found out it wasn't. I was miserable and thoughts of drinking came and went. Thankfully I had heard enough in the rooms to know there is no such thing as just the one for me. I have tried every way possible to drink successfully. I can't.

The Other Side

Being very close to relapsing in those months one day I sat on a bus and was considering getting off and going to a bar in Dublin city. I rang a friend who I knew had relapsed, secretly thinking she would give me the green light to go. She didn't! She said "*get your arse back round to the transition house.*" Another one of those moments for me when I could see clearly. I rang a staff member (who now happens to be one of my best friends) and told her I was having thoughts of drinking and she told me to go straight round which I did. I cried for hours. I cried because I knew that this was it, I knew it was time to do all the things I had been avoiding like getting a sponsor, getting honest and looking at the internal emotional stuff. I had to, my life depended on it.

That's exactly what I did, I got myself a sponsor and she's still my sponsor today. She tells me the truth and not what I want to hear. She's very direct with me and I appreciate and love her for that. I have a small circle of friends as I already mentioned, and I love them dearly.

I went to college to study addiction and as I got educated my recovery deepened. I also did recovery coach training in 2015 and I have to say for me this was more valuable than any diploma or degree. This training opened up my mind to other pathways to recovery because I pretty much had tunnel vision up until this point. I was a 12-stepper and thought this the only way. It is the only way for me and my personal recovery but I now accept it's not for everyone. I was introduced to others on a recovery journey through this training and my circle grew. I went on to work as a recovery coach in a transition house and was able to offer support to other women who I could identify with because I have walked a similar path. Some things never change though, I am still a grafter, and still work my way up to positions such as deputy manager of the transition house and now National Coordinator for the Academy. I'm now training new coaches and am able to support them on their journey. This all gives me a sense of purpose and belonging.

Everything that has happened over the last 11 years from transition housing, education, recovery coach training, employment and eventually getting my forever home, have all been like the building blocks of my new life. Ever changing, growing and strengthening.

Reflection

Looking back on my journey I see the importance on gender specific services. I didn't know it at the time but I knew that I had issues when it came to men. I didn't understand that the trauma I had experienced as a child, my biological father walking out on us shaped how I saw myself and how I formed relationships with men particularly romantic relationships. Don't get me wrong I had a wonderful stepfather from the age of 10 up and I loved him as much as I could but the early years without him definitely influenced my choices. I saw myself as unlovable, there was something wrong with me as a result of my father abandoning us, so I always went for the one who wasn't emotionally available or the one I couldn't have. Maybe it was the fact I had just turned 40 and had some level of maturity that I knew if I was going to get well, the only way I could possibly do it would be in an all-female environment. Whatever the reason is, today I understand the need for gender specific interventions and the importance they played in my recovery. I honestly don't think I would be here today without the female treatment centre and transitional housing. It was my safe space to start rebuilding my life without distraction.

As I write this now, I mentioned my sister Michelle earlier who passed away. Her inquest was held last week and I have been an emotional mess ever since. Death by misadventure. That is the reality of where addiction takes us. Although I am emotional, I have not once thought of trying to escape this pain by numbing it with a substance. That is the gift recovery has given to me, the ability to feel my emotions and sit with the pain. I know the intensity of this feeling will pass and I will find some peace again. I pray that in her honour I will continue to do so.

Do You Want a Cup of Tea... Before You Go

Sandra Losty

Today

I had the Sunday morning I used to dream about. I woke up slowly knowing there was no rush to get up out of bed. I lay still for a while so I could remember some of the dreams I had throughout the night. Snippets of a place I was in during my dream started to become clearer. I did not recognise the place, but I knew it. Something familiar was beginning to peep through and it was the feeling of the dream. I recognised the feeling of being lost and reminding myself that I am not lost, I've just never been here before. I enjoy trying to make sense of my dream state. Thankful that nightmares are rare now and that sleep is now something that supports me. There was a time in my life when being asleep was the most unsafe state for me to be in. But today the restful sleep I had was nourishing and replenishing. I was in no rush to get out of bed. I meditated a bit, said some prayers and took a blood pressure reading with a feeling of slight annoyance that I need to do this. It's "*just for now*" stop getting all worked up because you are now on blood pressure medication. It really irritates me that I have to take these tablets. I have always prided myself that I was the only one in my family who was not on any medication at all for anything! This was a serious blow to my pride that now I am the same as them. I was always the one who wanted to be different. Now I'll have to find something new to be different about!

But I digress. I woke up in a nice clean bed that had the bed linen changed on it yesterday and it felt so nice and cosy. I could feel the slight nip in the air now that there were more autumnal temperatures about. It always takes me a slow second to remember this is my house. I have half the mortgage paid on it and I have a car that was bought and fully paid for (a long time ago now) in the driveway. I have neighbours who say hello and pass the time of day with me when out and about and neighbours who when they knock on my door are asking me to hold the keys of their house in case they get locked out of their homes. Not once since I have lived here has a neighbour knocked in to ask me to lower the music or call the Gardí because of the shenanigans going on inside. Not one single time and I have lived here nearly 21 years. I got a mortgage when I was almost nine years sober. I had a full-time job and some savings to pay the deposit. I even had a friend who lent me some money to get the savings rolling so I could get a head start.

I actually have the life now that I dreamed of because I saw my friends have that life while I was still out there causing havoc. They were getting into relationships, getting married, having kids and building homes around themselves. There was a time I would say they were goody two shoes for conforming and convinced myself that they were the ones who were missing out. I also convinced myself that I was having a great time, even though hygiene habits like washing myself and having clean clothes to put on my body, had long since been a part of my life. I was the one who when I walked into the pub people averted their gaze and hoped I wouldn't sit beside them. I was a nightmare to sit beside. And here I am today with people actively seeking me out to help them. Every time something like that happens I hear a voice asking "*do they ACTUALLY know you*?"

Sometimes it feels like that voice doesn't know I have been sober for nearly 30 years and that I have changed significantly from those days where it was a day's work just staving off the voice that used to say relentlessly and with obvious tones of exasperation *"Just end it now. At least yer Da had the guts and he didn't even have a drink problem. You don't have to take someone with you like he did, just end yourself. You are as miserable as fucking sin!"* And that voice was right. I was as miserable as sin. There wasn't an ounce of joy to be found anywhere in my life.

The Old Days

I was in a relationship that centred around alcohol and the pub. It very quickly got to a point where we spoke two days of the week, the day he got paid and the day I got paid. We never went to the pictures (cinema) or out for a meal nor did we ever go for a walk just for the sake of going for the walk. The whole relationship was pub and alcohol centric. We drank with his friends who were old, like in their 40's and 50's. At least that's how I perceived them as I was 19 when we started going out and he was 10 years older than I was. Yet in some strange way they were a safety net. They in their own way looked out for me. Maybe I reminded them of their daughters.

My First Drink

But my problem drinking has its roots back to when I was 12 and I picked up my first drink. It was a cocktail of what was left in other people's glasses poured into a pint glass and hidden on the kitchen window sill. There was a party at our house on New Years Eve 1977. My aunt had come to visit from Australia with her 3 children to support my mother after the death of my father and sister earlier that year. This party was one of two parties I remember in my house with the other one being the hens party for my oldest sister Mary the year before. All the girls she worked with and the women around the area came in and great hooley was had. Her workmates made her an outfit and a big bonnet, and someone managed to find an old sun pram and they dressed her and pushed her around the area singing *"Going to the church and she's gonna get married."* There was great merriment around the place. She got hugged and kissed by everyone with the men telling her she will make a great wife cos she was a lovely girl (that was very true, and she still is) and the women saying "*run away, Mary run away*". The only man at that party was my dad who was out of hospital and he played "*bar man*". A table was placed across the kitchenette door, and he washed and dried the glasses as well as refilled them for everyone. All harmless fun and the kind of party that actually was a party in its full sense of the word.

They were the only two times that I recall volumes of alcohol being in my house growing up. We had the obligatory decanter of brandy and whiskey in the sideboard dresser (complete with a light in the drinks cabinet section of it) which only came out when visitors like aunts and uncles arrived. I don't think any of us actually realised it was alcohol and because we saw it so rarely it never dawned on anyone in the house to drink it. I know I genuinely saw the crystal decanters as ornaments. My mother loved her ornaments, and those crystal decanters were simply "*special edition*" ornaments.

So here at this New Years Eve party I find myself almost taking on my dad's role. Collecting and washing the glasses after I poured the remnants of the drink into that pint glass that was well out of view of anyone. I waited until it was almost full before I started to drink it. Up to that point I was bringing everyone a refill and keeping the general area tidy but that all stopped once I had it half finished. Very soon I was in blackout. The remainder of the pint glass was emptied, and I had started to simply drink from a bottle of beer with no fear for who saw me. I am not sure at what stage I started to vomit but when it did start it was like a fountain. I hated carrots and all I could see was carrots in what splashed on the ground as I puked. I actually got a bit distressed trying to work out where the carrots had come from! Somehow, I got to bed which spun like a fairground ride and that was a whole other level of distress and mental anguish.

However bad the night before was, it did not stop me the next morning when I went downstairs for a drink of water from picking up a can of beer that was open and drinking it. I have no idea why I did that. I certainly had never seen it in my home growing up. And thus, my fate was sealed. I got away with it. No one said anything to me and just like everything else of note that happened in the family we all carried on like it didn't.

My Drinking Continued

My first pub outing was after a session of roller skating a few months later. I got served at the bar at 12 years of age. It became a weekly thing and before long the roller skating didn't happen so we just went straight to that pub. I knew my mother's pattern of going to the bingo and I would arrive home just as she was going out. We sometimes brought some cans home and drank in my house. I would go to school reeking of booze and was at the centre of attention for being a daredevil for drinking. It was quite potent that feeling of being affirmed by my peers.

Losing My Mother

I left school at 15 years of age. Dying to get a job and earn a few bob for the drink. I was so done with babysitting to get some money. A job in a sewing factory came along and bingo. I was made up that I had my own money. My mother was a very shrewd woman and made me hand up half of my earnings which absolutely burst my bubble. She was trying to teach me that there is no such thing as an easy ride in life which was slowly dawning on me. She lived firmly by the *"It's far from your arse you won't sit on it"* philosophy meaning no matter what was wrong with you or in your life just get up and get on with it. But her untimely death when I was 16 put a stop to all that learning. I remember thinking quite soon after I realised, she was dead that I didn't have to hide drinking anymore!

From that day, to the day I had my last drink, the whole community became more aware I was drinking. I was a nightmare to be around. A glutton for the drink and the messes I got myself into. There are times I wonder how I made it out alive from the situations I found myself in. I was loud and brash and annoying. Slowly but surely my friends drifted away, and I started to drink on my own in my house. It was incredibly sad to look back and see that 17/ year old only able to focus on buying cans from the off licence. I descended into a monochrome life. I was either working in the factory or I was drinking on my own. There was no other activities happening in my life at all.

My First Boyfriend

I did manage to meet someone. He spotted me on the street and asked a neighbour about me who then set about bringing us together in the same place at the same time. That tornado of a relationship was to last for almost 10 years. We only ever went to the pub for nights out. We never once went to the cinema or out for a meal. He used to joke when we would go to the chipper on the way home from the pub that I could never say that he didn't treat me to world cuisine which was the Italian chipper and the Chinese takeaway.

That relationship over those 10 years descended into a place where the only feeling we had for each other was disgust and anger. There was no working on the relationship, there was only, who had money on any given day for drink. We argued like two people who hated each other. It got physical at times, and I was always blamed for what I made him do. He would feel guilty, I would feel like I had something over him and then the cycle would start all over again and we tolerated each other and the behaviours we engaged in to keep the drink flowing.

Seeking Refuge

Somewhere before the actual end of this relationship I had begun to seek refuge with my sister who lived out in the sticks as we called it then. And after a pretty serious incident I fled to her house for safety. I never once gave her a thought in all of this that the fall out of the incident might follow me out there. Fortunately for me (and her) it didn't, and I began to get some semblance of a life that did not revolve around going to the pub and drinking. She was very involved in holistic healing and held a reflexology workshop in her house for a friend who was training to become a reflexologist. She got some friends who were case studies for his accreditation and he did the sessions. I hate having my feet touched but went along with it to help out. I completely grimaced for every minute I was in the chair and was thrilled when it was over. We went to the pub that evening. Most people had two or three drinks and want home early and I stayed on lashing the bottles of cider into me feeling lightheaded from the first one. I had no concept that I had reduced my intake significantly over the time with my sister and literally poured several bottles of cider down my throat because I was "*thirsty*". We got an invite to a house party which I duly went to and downed a bottle of whiskey there. That resulted in me doing a "Sharon Curley" (this is a reference to a scene in the movie The Snapper where the main character vomits into her handbag) into my handbag. I have no idea how I got back to my sister's house but I woke up the next morning seeing my sister who died in 1977 in the corner of the room telling me *"You can't go out like that Sandra, you have a hole in the top of your head"*, I actually felt like my head was on the ceiling and my body was on the ground.

A Moment of Clarity

I was so frightened. I knew I couldn't go to collect my payment from the dole on my own, so I brought my 14-year-old nephew with me for safety in case anything happened to me. Once I got the money in my hands it was straight into the pub with the need for the hair of the dog and gathered momentum for my *"I'll show them"* attitude. Raging against the world with absolutely no reason for it. As the hours went by, my nephew was getting bored, I was getting irritated with him and sent him home on two buses back to where he lived (miles away) on his own with barely enough money for his bus fare. I thought it was 10 o'clock at night and I didn't care. That night was my last drink. I looked at the pint glass of cider and saw the top half of the glass was empty and I realised this is not working any more. I had a moment of clarity that I still feel when I think of it today. I asked a neighbour who I had seen putting his coat on to go home, could I walk up the road with him. That was the first time I had asked anyone for help other than to ask for money for a drink. I went back to the house I grew up in as I still had a key and when I woke up the next morning, I realised the danger I had put my nephew in by sending him home, that late at night on his own. I never felt as sick as I did when I recalled the look on his face when I told him I was sending him home. It haunted me. I knew in that very moment it was game over. I screamed up at God *"I can't fucking do this any more, help me"*. It was the most sincere request for help I had made in my entire life and I was 28 years of age at this stage.

I was still in my clothes from the day before. I got out of the bed, crept down the stairs and made my way back to my sister's house. This time it was me who barely had the money for the bus fare as I had spent most of it the day before. The journey back was excruciating. I spent all the time trying not to puke and at the same time trying to act normal. Although I had a key, I knocked on her door and when she opened it she said *"I hope you are here to pack your bags"*. I nodded my head defeatedly and went into the room to pack the clothes I had, all second hand, nothing I wore was bought by me as I didn't buy anything but drink with my money.

I couldn't find the words to say I am sorry for endangering your child or even ask if he was ok. After what seemed like an hour but in reality, was 2 minutes, she came into the room and the words she said sounded like a big church bell was clanged right beside my ear. *"Do you want a cup of tea BEFORE YOU GO?"* I could not believe she was putting me out on one hand and on the other it was the only thing she could do. I wanted to say, *"shove your cup of tea…"* but what came out of my mouth was what I believe to be divine intervention and I said, *"Yes please"*. When I sat in front of her I saw that pained look on her face and I knew it was me who had put that pained look on her face and I said to her with the same sincerity I screamed up at God earlier that morning *"Mary I know now what you have been saying to me all this time, once I start I can't stop"*. She cried, I cried and somewhere in the snots and tears I said I needed help and don't know where to start. I was 28 years of age, broken and broke and yet I felt a huge sense of relief.

Attending AA

Mary called someone who was in the AA fellowship and that person made arrangements for me to go to a meeting with another AA member. I heard in that room that very night a member sharing how he had lost his 3rd son to a drug overdose and how grateful he was to be able to be there for his family. I could not wrap my head around that. I thought if anyone needed a drink it was him! I saw right there and then as I shook and rattled because of yesterday's bender, there was something here that I had not seen or experienced before. It was enough to make me want to go back, and I have been doing so ever since. I stayed with my sister for about a year, and it gave a great sense of stability.

Rebuilding My Life

I got on a course (Soilse) and that introduced routine to me and a place to think about my future in terms of work. They had career guidance sessions, and I could explore this in depth. I wasn't sure what I wanted to do. I saw something about tourism and signed up for that. It wasn't what I thought it would be. More office based than travel based, and I went looking again. This time I saw something about family support and thought I'll give that go. I had no idea what I was stepping into. There were days I'd make my way over (2 buses) from one side of the city to another. I wonder *"what in the name of God am I doing on this work, how did I end up here?"*

I had been assigned to a family support service in one of the areas of Dublin that was most affected by the drugs crisis. I didn't feel skilled enough to help people. But I got great support from the team, and they really helped me drill down into what it was about the role I could do really well and identified what I needed to upskill on. I did a community development course and a drugs awareness course, and my confidence soared. It made crossing the city on two buses 5 days a week worth it.

The time came for me to move out of my sisters and live closer to town. I got a little bedsit flat so close to town that I could walk to work if I wanted to. I had saved enough for the deposit and for my first week's "*big food shop*". This was the first time in my life I had saved for anything and the first time I had ever lived alone. I was still on the back to work scheme, so I got government assistance to pay the rent. And as that scheme came to an end, I got my first salaried job which meant I was fully responsible for myself, my housing and my finances. It was 1997 and there were plenty of places to rent in Dublin that were affordable. As my job experience grew and salary increased, my housing improved. I could afford a nicer place each time. In comparison to my male peers in my 12-step meetings I found it easier to get accommodation than they did. Very often I'd hear they would need a recommendation from someone in the building before being considered as a tenant.

I also heard the women who had children also had difficulty getting accommodation because they had children. While I was grateful, I have a roof over my head I was incensed that this was happening. Oddly enough that first salaried job was with a service that provided information about rental accommodation and housing. We were surrounded by people who couldn't get accommodation. This was my first inkling around the topic of politics and economics. I didn't understand Boom times and crash times and how this affected the average person in society. I began to realise that somehow, I had managed to blend in. I wasn't sure how happy I was with that, but I was very happy not to be the one standing out for all of the wrong reasons.

Building Friendships

As time went by since that first meeting, I now had friendships in my life that I worked on and valued. All my childhood friends lived back in the area in which I grew up in and I avoided like the plague. We had drifted apart so many years ago anyway it didn't feel like a big loss, but I began to have regrets about how I was in those friendships. They were all now at this stage married and had families of their own. I envied them for that. I wished I had that path as well. I held deep sadness for that young girl who thought she was having a ball and thinking her pals were "*boring*" when all along she was doing the best she could at the time to survive and wasn't able to thrive.

So all of my friendships were now people in recovery and

some people I worked with became friends and I felt I was fairly balanced. We went to the cinema and had meals out in nice places. Apart from a sit-down chipper at the seaside I had never been in a restaurant. After meetings we would go to coffee shops and have cappuccinos and lattes which I disliked intensely and went back to drinking very strong tea, so strong you could stand a spoon in it. It was the freedom I had always wanted to be able to walk down the street and nobody paid any heed to me because I simply blended in. Until I laughed, then I got a lot of attention but other than that I did not stand out.

Feeling Free and Light

I had begun therapy. I had a sponsor who was very clear about the role of what a sponsor was and where to direct me when I presented to her things that went beyond that scope. I found I had a lot to unpack. To me it was all just things that happened. I didn't know I was still in survival mode. I felt so free and light, but therapy helped me understand me from different angles. It began to slowly dawn me that I had been through some shit, and I had avenues now to heal from it.

The Younger Sister I Never Had

I most definitely had good people around me who spent time with me just chatting or watching a movie on TV. There was no need for words of wisdom or advice, just simply being in each other's company helped to heal things they did not break. There is one friend whom I met in the workplace over 20 years ago and that friendship has been the backbone of all the joys and sorrows over that period of time. She has healed in me the deepest darkest wounds I have experienced in life none of which she caused, and I must include those wounds that happened even before I met her. My sanity would not have withstood what it had to withstand if I had not had her support. She is the younger sister I never had, the wise woman I have always needed and my biggest fan in all that I do. Friendships like this are once in a lifetime experiences and I treasure it as much as the air I need to breathe. I feel lucky to have her and other friends in my life and I work on maintaining these relationships.

I haven't yet managed to crack the secret to romantic relationships, so I have decided for this lifetime at least I am doing a solo journey. There are times I even believe I have such a big purpose to live that I would only get distracted having a man around. And on days I am really honest I know I am the biggest loner on the planet and would like to be living somewhere in the woods only seeing people when I absolutely have to and yet if you met me, you would describe me as a huge extrovert.

Trials and People Turning Up For Me in Beautiful Ways

I have had some amazing journeys in recovery. Life happened in a way that it did not happen when I was actively drinking. As a sponsor of mine once said *"There was no way you were going to find true love, earn a few bob for your future or make a positive difference in anyone's life when you were drinking flagons of cider in a field!"* How right she was because life has thrown me some challenges. In the first few years I had a string of events that came quite close together. The relationship I was in broke down and I became homeless. I got a new place to live shortly afterwards and in a period of 5 weeks I was mugged and ended up in hospital, was in a car crash (2 days later) on the way to an AA meeting and ended up in hospital and 4 weeks later my flat, my gorgeous little flat that I was only in for 6 weeks had a fire with me in it and yes I ended up in hospital! Some Karma clearing going on there! And here is what happened from people in the AA fellowship. They turned up with bags of clothes for me. Money in envelopes for me to replace what I had lost in the fire and someone I barely knew took me into their home until I found somewhere to live. People picked me up and brought me to meetings and dropped me back and helped me find new accommodation. My whole life turned upside down and it felt like I was starting all over again. In some ways I was starting over from scratch because losing everything except my life in a fire showed me things are replaceable, and people are my rocks. In a million years I never thought I would be one about whom people said, *"OMG how did you not drink?"* just like I thought hearing that man at my first meeting.

As time has moved on from the very early years of my recovery, I have gone back to education as a mature student to get a degree, and done some other professional development courses related to the work I was in. I have stayed in the social care field spending many years managing homeless services in the city centre. I have a fondness for delivering training and have designed and delivered some lovely training pieces that support workers in the field and more recently courses more specifically for people in recovery. When the pandemic hit, I opened an online space called Recovery Hour that is still going today. We have even met several times face to face over the last couple of years. I am always amazed at what we are capable of when we have to dig deep and show up for others and indeed ourselves.

Final Reflections

My final reflections are this. I have several main threads that are vital for me in my recovery. The first is the beautiful relationship I have with my sister. We have some laughs, and she tells me how proud she is of me. And alongside that relationship I have with my nephew who is now in his 40's and he too tells me how proud is of me. I send a prayer every day to heaven for them both and my niece too. They are who I consider my family.

I have only deepest gratitude for the 12-step programme that keeps my thinking on the straight and narrow and helped me build a relationship with God. Whenever things don't go my way, I only have to remind myself of that sequence of events around my last day drinking and my first day of recovery. I learned how to be a sister, an aunt, a friend and so much more because of it. Anywhere I go in the world I touch base with AA, not because I think I will drink but because it is a familiar experience in a strange land. The steps and traditions on the walls, the slogans on the table and the warm welcoming handshake. It still fills me full of joy and gratitude that I am a part of this fellowship. It also offers me the opportunity to give back to the newcomer who needs a warm welcoming handshake and reassurance that they are in the right place.

My friendship with my friend of over 20 years is such a richness in my life. It keeps me believing the world is a better place than my mind would have me believe. To have someone with whom you can be your true authentic self is a beautiful gift.

And last but not least my relationship with God to whom most of my prayers start with *"what the actual fuck...!"* sometimes said in jest and sometimes in desperation when I am struggling with living life on life's terms. I am truly blessed to have all these people and resources in my life who make me a better person and make life worth living and makes me want to continue fighting the good fight.

Discovery

Rubina Khan

Introduction

Writing this chapter fills me with anxiety and fear, emotions that I thought I had overcome after more than 20 years of recovery and working in the field of addiction. Yet, the stigma and shame surrounding addiction in the Pakistani community remain pervasive. This is one of the reasons I have dedicated over two decades to the recovery and addiction field. I am a mother, happily married to a supportive partner who fully understands the stigma that still exists in our community. This has inspired me to support and make changes for individuals in recovery or individuals that are in active addiction.

Growing up

But my journey hasn't always been this way. Born and raised in the UK, I struggled with my identity, trying to find a sense of belonging. At home, I was a Pakistani girl wearing salwar kameez (traditional Asian attire), which I also had to wear to school. This made me a target for bullying, with peers taunting me, "*Why are you wearing your mother's curtains*?" To fit in, I secretly acquired a pair of jeans and changed into them every morning in the public toilets. This small act helped me blend in with the crowd.

Arranged Marriage

As I progressed through school, my behaviour began to change. The community perceived me as becoming too Western. Consequently, at the age of 16, I was taken to Pakistan to marry my cousin. I lived there for just over a year with my husband, feeling lonely and frightened, away from my family and friends, and unable to communicate in English.

I didn't know how I did this, but I managed to adapt to my life in Pakistan I did find this difficult as I was not use to this way of life. The expectations were so different from being a Pakistani born and bred in the UK, the clothes I wore were accepted in Pakistan but the clothes I wore to school were not accepted, this was confusing I felt as though I did not feel I belonged in Pakistan or in the UK. When I was in the UK I was a Pakistani and when I was in Pakistan I was British, I started wonder about my identity and my sense of belonging. I felt as though I was living 2 worlds, this was hard for me to manage.

I returned to the UK to apply for a visa for my husband to join me. Two years later, he arrived, but he struggled to accept the British way of life, particularly the greater freedom women enjoyed. This led to him becoming controlling, and our marriage soon turned toxic and violent.

This was so difficult for us both manage there was no comprise as we both belonged in 2 different worlds. We tried to find common ground as we knew for the sake of my honour I had to stay in the marriage.

Becoming a Mother

A year later, I gave birth to my child. Eventually, I found the courage to tell my parents about the abuse I was enduring, but I could not tell them about my substance use, as I did not want to hurt them as they supported me through my divorce.

I managed to get a divorce but was left to raise my child alone. This was a daunting and lonely experience for me. During this time, a friend offered me substances to help cope with my fears. These substances became my comfort blanket, my new friends. However, they did not help with my finances, and guilt began to set in. I knew I should have been spending money on my child and home. I tried to stop using, but I soon realized I couldn't. I couldn't understand why. I had always thought I was stronger than this. Why was it so hard? I felt like I was victim again, but this time it was to something not a person. I felt like my life was spiralling, a divorce and now substances.

Isolation and Living in Fear and Shame

The worst part was that I had no one to talk to. I was terrified of the backlash or being ostracized by my family and community. I knew there were services that could help, but I was petrified someone would see me accessing a drug service. I could not find a way to support myself and get out of the crutches of addiction. I did not have the confidence to speak to my GP or the health visitor who visited me most weeks, I was scared if I said anything to my health visitor she will remove my child. Everywhere I turned there were barriers.

New Social Networks

Finally, I confided in a Caucasian friend. She advised me to attend a parent and toddler group to make connections, suggesting that this might help with the isolation I was feeling. While attending the group, I started to make positive connections.

Finding Meaning and Purpose

During this time, I met a lady who asked if I would volunteer for a women's group affected by a loved one's substance use. I jumped at the opportunity because it would help me in my own recovery and allow me to support other women.

The group was brilliant I met other women who experiences were like mine, which was a shock and a relief to me at the same time I thought this only happened to me, the group gave me a sense of belonging, and I found my place of safety. I also found structure and something that I was doing for myself and that I t was me time, at one f the session lady from a BAMER back ground attended after talking to her it was transpired that she was using drugs and came her as she was scared to use services for herself, from their I realised it was just not me who struggled to access mainstream drug and alcohol services. I connected with lady and we build a trusting relationship- we spoke to main street support service and we discussed concerns around women accessing services, they agreed to attend our group to offer support a safe environment, this felt like a break through, this also helped me with my recovery.

This role gave me a sense of purpose and set me on a mission to use my past experiences to make a difference for other women suffering in silence in BAMER (Black, Asian, Minority Ethnic, and Refugee) communities.

Reflections

Being a woman in the Pakistani community, I have experienced certain cultural barriers that had limited my ability to seek support. In the Pakistani community, it is uncommon for females to openly discuss issues around substance use, which created a sense of isolation and prevented me from accessing the supported I needed. On the other hand, males within our community are often provided with the necessary support and encouragement. This disparity highlights the need for more inclusive and understanding approaches that allow everyone, regardless of gender, to seek help and support.

If I had received the support I needed at the time, I wouldn't have faced the challenges that later affected my life. Eventually, I was diagnosed with anxiety and depression. When I went to my GP, I was offered antidepressants, but I refused them because I feared becoming addicted. I didn't want to swap one addiction for another. If I had been informed about what antidepressants were, I would have taken them, and it might have protected me from having two breakdowns. At one point, I even attempted to take my life; despite knowing it was forbidden in my religion, but I had needed the help, I was scared and alone, and at the time this was my only option to get myself out of this dark hole. I just wanted someone to say, "*you will get through this*" Deep down, I understood it was a cry for help. I believe that if I were a male, someone would have listened and offered some support.

Seeking Recovery as an Ethnic Minority

Rae Panache

My name is Rae Panache, I am a mixed-race woman with three children aged 24, 20 and 2. I am 11 years sober, 9 years clean and my recovery is a lifestyle I maintain every day. My father is Jamaican, my mother is British Caucasian and with me being born in England in the 80's I have been subjected to racism which has unfortunately been part of my journey. I will be sharing some experiences of this in relation to my recovery journey, how I've been made to feel personally, and how my race has stopped me from excelling in certain areas of my life, education, employment etc.

I am not one to bring out the race card when I have not been granted the opportunity to obtain things and I will give clarification so you will see the implications of the avenues I took to better my life. I have to laugh and be thankful that I have an All-Mighty Creator that has blessed me with a sense of humour because as they say if you don't laugh you will cry. My resilience has been tested in many ways.

Today I am grateful. I have a beautiful family I see grow and flourish every day. I am in a much better place mentally, physically, emotionally and spiritually. I am following my dreams and pursing ambitiously a career as an entrepreneur with my own social enterprise ERA, Educational Respectful Attitudes. I am an author and have written about my alcoholism called Dr Jekyll and Madame Rose. I have combined my academics along with my lived experience to be able to create bespoke workshops, projects and programmes that I feel are needed especially in socially deprived areas and for those of ethnic origin.

Before I set out to develop ERA, I did a lot of voluntary work in different communities and organisations. I helped deliver the Drug and Alcohol Prevention programme with The Amy Winehouse Foundation, Volunteered with Project 6 and did a few training programmes with Waypoint. I have sat on research panels, one being SHARRP. I have travelled to different cities to do motivational talks and share my experiences of my recovery both in mental health and addiction. Doing all these things has given me a sense of purpose and in sharing our stories we can give people the hope they need to make changes for themselves. I am all about empowering others.

I feel proud of my accomplishments that I have made whilst being in recovery, I have learnt so much about myself and the world around me. I have developed tremendously and have so much depth and understanding when it comes to how my mind works. I throw myself into education, as they say knowledge is power, but it doesn't mean much if you are not applying to your life, that is where you become wise. One of my favourite quotes is, to be old and wise, you have to be young and foolish.

I lost a lot whilst I was in active addiction, my children for a brief amount of time, my freedom, due to serving a sentence in prison, my mind, due to my poor mental health and family and friends along the way. So, I am all about the gains in life.

I keep my circle small, and I can count my friends on one hand, people come and go in life, and this was evident in my life in active addiction. I am all about quality over quantity and that's keeping it real. Misery loves company. My social circle has always been one of genuine friendship between friends, neighbours, and colleagues. Love thy neighbour is what I stand by, yet I have had to learn the hard way in some relationships with others as I have a big heart, and I can say that back in my active addiction days I was gullible, trusting and loyal to people who never returned that same type of energy. I have been in positions where friends and strangers have taken advantage of me, and this has been a huge lesson that I have learned along my journey. Hand on heart I forgive anyone who has ever done me wrong, and I am a big believer that our biggest mistakes become our greatest lessons.

I will be sharing my personal experiences and perspectives of my recovery through communities, meetings, and the support that was available as a service user and volunteer.

I have always been the only ethnic minority in recovery meetings. Addiction does not discriminate. You could be rich or poor, young or old, from different genders, sexualities and ethnic backgrounds etc. So, why is it that within these recovery spaces there is an extremely low percentage of the BAME community not accessing services and treatment? This baffled me along my recovery journey because I always seemed to be the only minority at meetings, the rest of the group were predominantly Caucasian. There was a mixture of genders both male and female and over time I was aware that these groups evolved as women only groups and men's groups.

Recovery from the perspective of a woman will raise its own issues. Women may need to raise very upsetting and personal issues such as sexual assault or domestic violence and they would need a space to feel comfortable to share their experience and the same goes for men if they want to talk about things in more depth like their mental health or prison sentences etc. So, I do understand the need for specific groups to tackle or express some of their issues that may be connected to their recovery journey. This has been the case for the LGBT, and they have set specific meetings to accommodate around them, yet ethnic folk have been addressed last. There are all sorts of barriers to accessing help and support and looking at cultural barriers really needs some research and time spent on addressing this.

Being the only person of ethnicity in group meetings never deterred me from my recovery path, I kept my focus because the main reason why I was there was because I acknowledged and accepted that I had a problem and needed help. This seemed to be the only place that I would get the support I required. I needed help and my only solution came in the form of organisations that were predominantly run and used by Caucasians. However, during meetings I knew there were certain topics and issues that I could not disclose or express due to most people in the meeting not having a mutual understanding of the types of experiences I'd faced as an ethnic minority.

From 2009 to 2024 I have always been aware of the lack of ethnic representation. I would also like to mention that no one has ever made an issue of my race within these groups, I have never felt discriminated against, and I have always felt like I was treated equally. I got the same support and guidance as everyone else. Although, there was a time where I felt like I was a "*token*" in the recovery community as the Equality and Diversity regime was very much being looked at within organisations. I felt that organisations were putting images of ethnic representation on leaflets and websites to get ethnic people to come through the doors, but it was like a falsity because as soon as this ethnic group were to come through those doors that ethnic representation was not there. Could you imagine what thoughts may go through one's head at that moment. For me it would be I've been lied to, deceived.

Equity is about fairness and justice and not all of us start from the same place, we must look at how far black people have come in terms of oppression and discrimination that they have faced for many years. The issues we currently have today could possibly be rooted from slavery. The trans-Atlantic slave trade was the largest forced migration in human history and although it predates all the way back to 1600's it went on for many years. The amount of damage that has caused to that group of people is inexplicable. Moral implications of slavery and the severe brutality of these people were only looked upon from the late

1700's and was abolished in the 1800's but it didn't end there. Black people were enslaved well into the 1960's, have fought for equal rights and opportunities but this is not a write up on black history I merely want to add a little perspective as to one of the reasons this group of people don't access treatment or services in the recovery community. There will be other reasons that need to be explored but let us move on.

I Stepped Back From the Recovery Community

I ended up removing myself from the recovery community because I never felt understood especially when it came down to the type of discrimination I had received because of my ethnicity, social status, past and lack of cultural understanding. I had always talked about diversity within the recovery community but was never really heard. I was enthusiastic about providing workshops and delivering them which got overlooked and felt that writing a book and setting up a social enterprise to engage on a more professional level was a waste of time for a couple of years and it did get to the point where it affected my mental health. Fortunately, my recovery game was so strong I never dithered back into active addiction. Rejection can be a huge kick in the gut and can make a person decline in all sorts of ways.

It isn't that Black, Asian, or other ethnic minorities are not allowed to access this space. All individuals are accepted regardless of their race, status, class etc so it just poses the question as to why they do not seek intervention within the recovery community.

2010 was the year that I actively started working on my recovery. I was allocated a support worker and attended SMART meetings. I have never felt a real sense of belonging within a recovery community so I would shy away from really embedding myself within the structures of that community. Its only recently that I attended a Recovery Celebration event, and

I am so glad that I did as I heard talks of inclusion and a real urge to make all people from all walks of life to get involved and be a part of a city that promotes equality, inclusion and diversity. This is where I was given the opportunity to express my views in this book.

Cultural barriers faced are notably a challenge for those who are part of an ethnic minority group. From the language and non-verbal communication used as this can lead to misunderstandings. I have been in this situation before, and I have been told that I come across intimidating or aggressive. When I express myself, I tend to use my hands, my body language is very assertive, and I may talk in my native tongue, patois.

Society Mirrors Recovery Communities

This casts my mind back to when I was receiving treatment for my Bipolar condition. Being the only black family on the block could only mean trouble! I have the utmost respect for this Caucasian male CPN worker who supported me with my mental health during 2009-2012. He saw that I was being subjected to prejudicial behaviour from neighbours and staff within the housing office and I appreciate that he noticed and mentioned that due to my cultural background that I was being judged and stereotyped. At this time, I was also trying to help my adolescent son who was going down the wrong path. I sought out intervention with a youth prevention team and as I was in early recovery I felt like everything was testing me. I had a great guy who worked with my son who was Asian, and he totally understood and came with a non-judgemental attitude. He was a great help for my son during his troublesome times.

My CPN wrote on my behalf and said that I was a lovely person who was doing all the right things and that if the neighbours in the block were to get to know me then maybe they would see things differently, but people's preconceived notions, assumptions or negative images about my culture already had created a huge barrier.

I was open to communicate with my neighbours even though I was being judged by them and I was never disrespectful to any of them. I received a lot of complaints whilst I lived in my flat due to the music I played, the food I cooked and about the people that came to my flat. They didn't like my son or his friends which are also mixed race and black. Yet, this was also my home; I shared a communal space with my neighbours, and I just had to overcome these judgemental people and get on with my life. It has been something I have been accustomed to most of my life anyway, so I took it with a pinch of salt. I can't be liked by everyone, and eventually I ended up moving from my 2-bedroom flat into a 3-bedroom house in a more diverse area.

Family Dynamics and Support Systems

My support systems were not my strong point, so I always relied on third parties in the form of social and mental health services. I am the 4th eldest of 19 siblings and as my mother was adopted when she was born, I didn't have the usual dynamics of a loving family with Grandparents, Aunties, Uncles and cousins and this was the case on both sides. All my father's side of the family resided in Jamaica. This is why I heavily relied on third parties such as the social services for help and intervention. I was open and honest about my substance misuse and there were no issues regarding neglect around my children as I was a functioning addict. The kids were always at school on time, well presented and there were no reports of ill treatment. When my social workers came round, they were more than happy with my living conditions and were very supportive. They would praise me for being a good mum despite having the issues I had, and they could see that I provided a loving home for them. They knew about my childhood and that it wasn't the norm, and they liked how aware I was and how I shared my experiences.

For me it's always being about breaking generational curses and with my mother being an alcoholic who never sought help I could see the similarities between us. This only made me want to seek help as I didn't want to be anything like her. So cold, unloving and reserved. Growing up having to witness so much domestic violence really made me know that I wasn't going to allow anyone to put me in that position. I wouldn't want my children to witness such things and all I ever wanted was a safe environment for them to thrive in. I travelled to many cities with my mother. We were in hostels and safe houses, and it was only up until I was a teenager that she finally settled back in our hometown of Sheffield.

As she was so emotionally absent from her children due to her own traumas and alcoholism it was so easy for my mother to kick me out of the family home at the age of 14. So, I was a teenager living in the adult world from a very early age with no support from no one. Its no wonder that I became a young teenage mum. I really believed at the time that I was going to be the best mum ever and give my children the love that a child deserves. Only I was struck with postnatal depression soon after the birth of my first-born son. I couldn't help feeling distant from my child and I really felt like I was like my mother in this aspect. I saw myself drinking in an unhealthy way and I always thought this was exactly the way my mother coped. I was in total conflict with my feelings. The only difference was that I sought out the help I needed, got a diagnosis and worked through my feelings of emptiness.

On reflection, I have always loved my son, it was just the intensified feelings and doubts in my head along with Post Traumatic Stress Disorder (PTSD) that made it seemed so hard. My siblings have always said that I was very protective over my son, but it was just so difficult as I felt like I didn't have a maternal bone in my body and loving someone when you have come from an unloving environment didn't help. I'm happy to say that me and all my children have a fantastic bond and relationship and

I'm the type of mother that is there for her children through the good, the bad and the ugly. Yet I really feel deeply for my mother that she never could have a relationship with any of her children and as time past she left Sheffield on her own and she doesn't know any of her grandchildren. As a parent you don't get a guidebook, and it is one of the hardest jobs anyone can have.

Again, is this the damage caused through her being adopted and having no connection to family roots? All I can do is pray for her to find peace and I do forgive her for not being there at times where I needed a mum. I was a little lost girl seeking love in all the wrong places and getting up to all sorts of fuckery. I was raped at the age of 15 and had no-one to confide in, I had no family support system. This was something I had to just accept that happened to me and I just said to myself I shouldn't have been where I was at that time. I was in the clubs, drinking and doing drugs with adults and this happened in a flat I went back to. I just felt numb. I was in shock but just carried on with my life sleeping from couch to couch up until I got into a hostel at the age of 16. At that point I felt safe and secure and not under anyone's thumb.

My First Recovery Meeting

My first ever recovery meeting was with Alcohol Anonymous (AA) in Drakehall prison in 2008. This was my first and will be my last incarceration. Before I was incarcerated, I read a lot of self-help books to try and understand myself and my behaviour. I never saw my use or behaviour as a problem because drinking and doing drugs were so normalised in my world/ neighbourhood. It seemed that everyone was doing it. I come from a socially deprived background with a mixed heritage. The way I look has always raised questions, as I was mixed, I was referred to as black or Asian and ever since being a little girl I can remember enduring racial slurs and I was only ever trying to fit into society. This was very hard for me as I am English, born and bred, so being told by people to go back to your own country shocked me. Are people really that ill-educated to say such things? So, yes racism was very much prevalent in my days growing up and still is unfortunately in these present times.

I knew I had an issue with the drinking and the drugs, I felt ashamed of myself that I allowed things to get this far where I was locked up and away from my children. This was the first time that I ever had the notion that I might have been an individual with an alcohol and substance misuse problem. The poisons of my choice were cocaine, alcohol, ecstasy, Ganja and amphetamines and my alcohol and drug use started at the age of fourteen.

At these meetings I would sit openly and confess to other inmates that I was an addict and that I had a problem. It was the first time that I had addressed my issues out loud to others and it was here that I found out that I wasn't the only one who had substance misuse issues. I was never offered these meetings during my stay in Newhall prison and looking back now I felt like there wasn't enough support for people with issues of active addiction or mental health.

I didn't quite understand what the 12-step programme was, I never fully read the leaflet or absorbed the fundamental principles of recovery, I just went along with weekly meetings whilst I served my sentence. I served a 6-month sentence and as soon as I was released it wasn't long before I slipped back into my old ways. The first thing I did when I got out of prison was buy two miniature bottles of white zinfandel on the train at 7.20 in the morning. The meetings obviously did not have an impact on me.

Luckily, I still had my home to go back to when I got out of prison and my focus was getting my children back home as they had been staying at their grandmothers with their dad. I knew that their dad wasn't going to make it easy for me and just hand them over. So, we went to court over a residency order and because I had fixed abode, and he did not want the children returned into my care.

I continued living in active addiction, displayed more problematic behaviour, presented trouble with my mental health and ended up back on probation. My life became chaotic and hectic once again because of my substance abuse.

Working on My Recovery

It was the year 2010 and I knew that I needed to find a support group, so I found a local AA meeting at a church in the city centre. It was more overwhelming attending an AA meeting the second time round rather than the first time, and I think this was due to sourcing the help myself and it being outside of prison. I was voluntarily seeking the help I needed and being in a circle talking about these very sensitive issues around my alcohol and drug use really helped give me insight into my thoughts, feelings and behaviour. I knew that what I needed wad some form of intervention as I couldn't do this on my own. I had to admit this to myself all over again and there was no way that I was going to lose my freedom through active addiction.

I tried AA meetings a couple of times before I was introduced to SMART meetings. A woman told me about an organisation named SASS that worked with people who wanted a life in recovery, she said they held similar meetings, provided you with a mentor for 1-2-1 support, an individualised plan, access to drop in with all sorts of activities and formed what was called a recovery community. It all sounded very professional. In AA meetings I didn't feel comfortable having a sponsor as I had trust issues and was currently working through present and past traumas. I was not about to confide all my problems to someone I hardly knew.

I spent a good 9 months with SASS attending weekly meetings and having my 1-2-1s with my mentor/support worker. This was the time I took my recovery seriously, No room for denial. Just straight up acceptance and a route out of addiction. I was sick and tired of being trapped in a world of undesirable habits, insane thoughts, and prone to risky behaviour. The instability of my reality and my mind made me come to terms with the fact that I was a problematic substance misuser. I had a great rapport with my support worker and really felt that these meetings were working for me. My recovery was my only interest once I arrived at the centre, I was serious about living a life in recovery and remaining abstinent. I wasn't there to engage with any of the drop ins or activities, I never felt like needed to be part of a recovery community and it never crossed my mind that it was due to the lack of representation of people like myself. These group meetings served a purpose and kept me away from alcohol and drugs, such a live saver in my eyes.

Looking back now perhaps it might have had some connection to being the only person within meetings that was an ethnic minority. Week after week I would notice this, and I'd question in my own mind why this was. There wasn't anyone available to me that I could have this conversation with. I was in a room full of Caucasians who wouldn't know of any of my experiences due to my race, racial profiling, racism, education, employment, cultural background etc.

I am a person who enjoys speaking openly and honest about my life and my use. Sharing the deepest, darkest facets of your being, sharing your thoughts, feelings and actions is a huge thing to do especially within groups. You may feel misunderstood or judged and I guess that is part of the process.

Racial Profiling by the Police

Whilst living in a predominantly white area where I was the only ethnic person living in that block of flats. I lived on the middle floor, and I really was keeping my head down and staying out of trouble. I heard some commotion outside my block, looked outside and saw that the neighbours were arguing. It was getting very heated so I decided to go down and see if I could de-escalate the fight and be a peace maker. I told everyone to calm down, there was loads of screaming and shouting and I obviously had to raise my voice also to be heard. I got in the middle of two individuals to stop them getting physical with one another and whilst I was calming the situation down the police had arrived due to someone calling them out about the disturbance. Straight away they approached me, man handled me down to the ground and handcuffed me. I was shocked as I was not the problem, and I was there to help.

My neighbours continued shouting but now they were shouting at the police to make them understand that I'd just come out the flat to calm things down and that the argument did not concern me. This did not deter them, and I was thrown into the back of a riot van, taken to the police station where they booked me in, then charged with a public order offence. This was all I needed whilst I was trying to stay clean and sober Another charge on my head!

It was the year 2011 and at the time I was fighting for my children in court over a residence order. I was in early recovery and really didn't need the stress of this whole scenario. I had been racially profiled. There was no one I could talk to about this matter and in black and white my life just looked like disorder and chaos. It was a very challenging time for me. I didn't even feel like I could go back to meetings in the recovery community to seek the help I required. I just declined mentally, physically, emotionally and spiritually. I had no faith and hope in my situation. I viewed myself as a hot mess that was a total fuck up. With court and this incident that occurred I saw myself relapse once again. I got to the point where it all seemed pointless. Why was I fighting for my children when deep down I felt like a failure and obviously had poor coping mechanisms and mental health?

It was the second time that I was in court regarding my children. The first time was when I came out of prison, and like I said, I plummeted back into a chaotic world of active addiction which then saw me lose my home, sense of direction and children. I handed my children over to their father voluntarily as I did not want them to live in a hostel as I, myself grew up living in many hostels with my mother as a child. I made the conscious decision to go into a hostel on my own, get rehoused, sort out my mental health and get my children back once I was re-homed.

My son came back to live with me after residing with his dad for a year and a half, but I had to wait was 4 years before my daughter came to live with us. I had to wait until my children were all the age of 12 and for them to be Gillick competent, hence being able to speak for themselves, and both my children wanted to be at home with their mother.

Final Thoughts and Reflections

In conclusion the cultural barriers faced and experienced by those of ethnicity needs to be researched in more depth. Campaigns and discussions will only help tackle these issues which I believe need to be led by people that represent their ethnic group. We must come to an understanding that those who are not from an ethnic minority group would not face some of the prejudices and discrimination as those that do. I have faith in 2024 and many futures to come that we will see a more inclusive recovery community that includes all walks of life. Until then a space needs to be created for them in order to reach this place of inclusivity. If there were more job opportunities and prospects for those of ethnicity to work alongside existing recovery organisations, then I am sure that this would make a recovery community more appealing to them as they would feel a sense of ethnic representation.

It would be a great move forward if cultural awareness/educational content could be added to recovery programmes as this awareness may be what is needed for this group to feel included and valued as a member of the wider community and within an inclusive recovery community.

Taking My Power Back

Rita Nangle

Introduction

I'm Rita, a 56-year-old woman of Caribbean heritage. I am still fairly early on in my recovery, but life now looks so different. I am not the same person I used to be. I have so many amazing friends and have got to do so many amazing things that I never thought I would be able to do. I am so grateful for everything I have in my life. It is unrecognisable to my life before.

Childhood

I'm originally from Nottingham where I grew up in a large family with my mum, 3 brothers and 1 sister. I had a good childhood. However, my father was very strict and abusive. My mum tried many times to leave him many times because of his violence towards her and us kids but there was no support or refuges around back then. Even the police wouldn't help until finally mum got an injunction against him. By this time I was aged ten.

My mum worked two jobs to afford a house, and we moved to a small town on the outskirts of Nottingham. We were the only black family in the area.

At school, I was a good athlete, and became the fastest runner in the region. I even trained with Seb Coe during my teens.

However, by age 17 I'd had two kids. Their dad moved away to Antigua. After that I fell into a relationship with a very abusive man. I'd grown up believing that abuse and violence was normal.

I ended up taking a wrong path in life and found myself in some very dark places. I was in so much pain. I lashed out and argued with everyone, thinking I could pass that pain on.

My Healing Journey

Eventually I came to understand that no one else could feel my pain, no one else could speak for me and that was when my healing journey began. I now have my eyes wide open; I can see more clearly, and I know what I want from life in recovery. Drugs and alcohol held so much power over me. I was a prisoner to them. I didn't know when or how I could be set free until I realised only I could free myself.

There have been relapses and lapses, I won't deny that, but I have the best support now and I have learned to love and forgive myself. I've also learned to forgive the people who hurt me, so I no longer have my back to the future. I can walk forward with hope and pride.

These days my life is busy and fulfilling. I went to college to become a Peer Mentor and a recovery ambassador. I'm a volunteer for project 6, an associate with the Changing Futures programme at South Yorkshire Housing association and I fund-raise for the children's hospital. I'm hoping to return to college in the future to study maths, English and business so that I can pursue my dream of running my own charity. I believe that we should never turn our back on anyone as people once did to me. Therefore, I want to call my charity "*don't turn your back*"

I'm determined to keep up the fight to stay clean and sober.

Women Supporters

I made many attempts to get clean through detox and rehab, but it wasn't until I moved to Rotherham and then Sheffield in 2022 that I was able to make real progress. I was at the Greens for 1 year and 3 months and I loved every moment there. I made many positive connections with others in recovery. My keyworker Cathy was great and of dual heritage also. This meant a lot as the recovery spaces are often wholly or majority white spaces. I met Tracey Ford who welcomed me into the recovery community with open arms. I'd been in a terrible state at the beginning. I was so thin and sick. Yet Tracey saw something good in me. She never judged. She always gave great advice. She was like a sister.

Other positive influences in my recovery have been the staff and volunteers who've supported me along the way; Louise at the Greens, Lyndsy at the Priory, Manya and Becks at project 6. These women nurtured and supported me to learn and try things I didn't believe I could do previously. I found the courage to do online training courses and passed them all. I started going to meetings and speaking up when in the past I'd believed I didn't belong there.

The Power of Hope

At the Greens I met people who were turning their lives around and leaving their addictions behind them. They inspired me and made me even more determined to pursue a new and better life.

The Power of Family

After so many failed attempts at detox and rehab, my immediate family began to lose hope. It was my cousin, my aunts and my nan who first stepped up to support me when they believed I'd made the firm decision that enough was enough, and it was at last the right time.

A drug worker in Nottingham made the call. My cousin Richard gave me all the practical help to move myself and my stuff in. Along with Aunty Sandra, Aunty June, Aunty Yvonne and Uncle Gary, they visited and supported me. Their encouragement showed that they wouldn't give up on me.

Overcoming Obstacles

As a black girl living with a strict father, I was forced to hide my addiction. Both my parents told me that only white people use coke, crack and heroin. I would visit London and do coke at weekends then return to Nottingham and act as normal. I only ever used with white people but I soon realised that black and Asian people were also forced to hide their addictions from their families and communities due to the stigma.

Stigma

I couldn't use the services in Nottingham due to the shame and stigma my family felt. They were well known in the Caribbean community. My dad was a chef, and my uncle owned the community centre.

When my father found out he sent me to Canada to stay with an uncle. I was escorted everywhere and was never allowed to be on my own except to go to the toilet and to bed.

Being Black in a White Space

Throughout my years of addiction, I struggled to approach or engage with services because there were so few women of colour. Being a black woman meant people saw and treated me differently. I was perceived as loud and aggressive when I tried to express myself and my pain. No matter your race or religion, addiction doesn't discriminate but some people in services do.

Reflections

I often wonder if I had to go on this journey to get to where I am now. I have taken many different roads; some winding, some straight, some very dark. They say your future is unwritten and you can write your own story. There will always be good chapters and bad ones. It's how you deal with them that matters most. I needed to take my power back from drugs and alcohol. I was determined to do that with love in my heart and love for my life.

Do you remember the song "*He's got the whole world in his hands?*" We do have the world in our hands as humans. Small things to some people are big things for others. It's what we do in this world and for one another that matters.

Renewed Hope

Alison Thornhill

My name is Alison. I am in my 50's, I have a job, a long-term relationship and own my house. From around 2010 to 2019 I had a secret alcohol addiction. I was what is called an alcoholic; however, I like to use the term high functioning alcohol dependant.

Since being in recovery have gained so much in the last 5 years within my recovery circle. I am not saying I am cured but I am happy, enjoying life and most of all I like myself.

I am involved in volunteering within the recovery community by helping individuals. This involves facilitating support groups and I have also volunteered for an organisation to help other organisations obtain funding for positive activities and spoken at Recovery events about my experience.

I now work in Alcohol Services which is a dream come true. I am now helping others who have a problem with alcohol, letting them know they can get help and there is no judgement. Some of the people I work with are very poorly and some are suffering with end of life. Having lived experience has helped me tremendously. Helping other individuals fighting their demons. Knowing the pitfalls, getting them involved in other activities. I believe it's not just about giving up the drink, you have to be honest and work on yourself in order to succeed. I like to call it the real me, it does take an awful lot of reinventing the person I was before the addiction.

I have been a qualified S.M.A.R.T facilitator for the past 3 years. SMART stands for Self-Management and Recovery

Training. These meetings deal with the here and now and can cover absolutely anything providing it is recovery related. This can be thoughts, feelings, urges, triggers and the list goes on. Facilitating these groups helps not only others but myself. It is rewarding as you see people come for their first meeting broken and needing help. Over time they begin to change both mentally and physically and learn to live again.

So here is where I started off and where I am now.

Recreational Use

My love of mind-altering substances started with the rave/ dance scene in the late 80's/90's and this is where I met my long-term partner Dan in 1996. By the early 2000's I had given them up completely and was living a "*normal*" life. Occasionally having cannabis for a couple of years after the clubbing had finished. I would not call this experience as being addicted to a substance. I could take it or leave it no problem.

I was in my early 30's when I started drinking, a social drink after work, special occasions and some good nights out, it was not a problem, and I could take it or leave it. I was a social butterfly. The best person to be around, I was fun and had so much confidence.

Unprocessed Grief of Losing my Dad

At 35 this was a poignant age for me for the following reasons. My father had died when I was very young. I was 4 years old, and he was only 35 years old when he passed away. My mother brought myself and my 2 older brothers up together by herself and whilst I am not going to say it was easy, we always had food on the table, clean clothes, a warm house and holidays each year. Mum never told me she loved me and never discussed "*dad*" and I never mentioned Dad. This is where my thought processes and reactions were different from other people and the alcohol quietened my head and pushed those emotions down.

At this time, I was thinking I never knew him, I couldn't remember anything about him, and I didn't want to ask mum as I worried I might upset her.

Then it progressed onto having alcohol in the house, picking up a bottle of wine on my way home. This was helping me unwind and relax after a long day at work and to get to sleep at night.

I then moved onto a bottle of wine and half a bottle of vodka with diet coke this is what gave me the buzz I needed. I was still being a social person and keeping in contact with my friends/family and attending work on a regular basis. I was still running the household. Cleaning, cooking, washing clothes and paying bills. I went into a spiral of not addressing my mental health and finding solace in a bottle. It made me forget about the thoughts and feelings I was experiencing: The main one was that I was not good enough, I had to be 100% in everything I did. 100% at work, people pleasing, of course now I know now I was setting myself up to fail everyone makes mistakes, life is a learning process. Loneliness even when around people, wondering what my life would be like with Dad around. Along came self loathing, self pity, anxiety and depression and no confidence at all in myself.

Escalating Problematic Use

Not long after my 35th birthday, the purchase of wine stopped, and I was drinking vodka. No point in mixing the drinks and I was finding white wine a little sweet. This was the start of cancelling nights out or special occasions with friends and family. I was drinking in the comfort of my own home. No judgement just me and what was turning in my best friend "*Vodka*". I had progressed onto nearly a full bottle of vodka a night starting as soon as I got home from work. My partner worked different shifts to me, and I would be in bed by the time he got home. He had no idea just how much it had escalated in such a short space of time.

I was experiencing withdrawals at work and shaking in the mornings, but I never thought I was addicted. Addiction only effects the homeless and it is a legal substance.

In 2017 I watched a programme "*drinking into oblivion*" it was regarding people who were addicted to alcohol showing the effects it can have on your body. It followed a vodka drinker, he drank the same as I and it showed you the withdrawals etc, I remember thinking "*I'm not as bad as him*" but really, I was.

The drinking in the morning started because this stopped my withdrawals, this was when I had moved to part time working so I knew exactly how much I needed to get to work, and providing I was home by 3pm I could control my withdrawals. Panic would set in if I had not got enough for the morning. This is the time I realised I could not afford the amount I was spending on alcohol. Everything in my day was planned right down to me drinking, it was like a timetable and by this time I had been having at least one bottle of vodka a day for the past 12 months.

I didn't want Dan to know how much I was spending on vodka so I thought I would pay for 1 bottle and shoplift the other. This went on for several months. I was in the throes of surviving on vodka, hardly eating anything and never being sober just topping up all the time. It was starting to affect my work, self-care and relationships.

Recovery Supports

I would not be where I am in my recovery without a range of things that helped me along the way.

The Life Changing Interaction With a Security Guard Who Caught Me Shoplifting

I finally admitted defeat in April 2019. I had gone into my usual shop to purchase one bottle and to shoplift the other. I did my normal routine paid for one bottle at the checkout and then left the store. Once I had got about 3ft away from the door I heard someone behind me, the security guard had followed me, and I got caught shoplifting a bottle of Vodka. He escorted me back into the shop and took me up the escalators to a room and we waited for a female to arrive. The security guard gave me a dressing down, saying I had a drink problem, he asked did I have children, a job, a home? He stated he had seen me before. To be fair he probably had done, this wasn't the first time I had shoplifted, it was the first time I had got caught. He said if I carried on drinking, I would lose everything. He asked if I had shoplifted anywhere else and said he would find out. He repeated over and over about me looking like an addict. I denied, replying I had anxiety and depression, and this is why I looked like this. I burst into tears, and I mean into tears. Remember when you were little and you sobbed and had to catch your breath, this was me. This is when the female said to stop because I was so upset. What I had done was not in line with my values, how I had been brought up. I thought about my mum and Dan how disappointed they would be in me and how I had let them down. He told me I would not be arrested I would receive a fine. He didn't know how much. He then asked if I would like some help and through my tears, runny nose I said yes. This was the first person who helped me on my road of recovery, and I really mean this from the bottom of my heart, and he gave me the details of SASS (Project 6). This was an organisation who helped people in addiction and was local to me. The following day I rang the organisation to see about seeing somebody, I was still drinking and at this time I knew it was the drink enjoying me, more than me enjoying the drink. I was just drinking to survive. I had no self-care and was hardly eating instead I was drinking empty calories. I knew I had hit my rock bottom. I rang and was invited down by a kind gentleman who answered the phone, I remember saying to him when he answered, "*I need some help with my drinking*" to which he replied "*you have called the right place*". I went down to see them that afternoon. I was a little nervous but has usual I had, had my quota of vodka before attending. I stalled at the entrance but then rang the buzzer, I was in the building I was taking my first steps. It felt good in a funny sort of way. I was addressing my addiction.

I spoke to a lady called Helen who told me what they actually did. I cried all the way through telling my story and how I ended up there asking for help. There was no judgement, no shocked face and I felt safe there. Not only did they help with sobriety they also help with activities and meetings. I booked an appointment with a recovery worker for 1 week later. I was invited to the ladies SMART meeting on the bank holiday Monday, and I thought I would give it a go. You see as an addict you certainly don't expect kindness from strangers, because this lady had gone through addiction herself, she understood what the madness was like, the lying, deceit and we will do anything to get our drug of choice. She got it because she had the life experience of addiction.

Getting the Help I Needed

The following day I went to see my doctor to get a sick note for work. I told my doctor everything, and received a sick note, and a prescription for strong vitamin D tablets and thiamine, they also took FLT blood tests from me as well. When I received the results, I was told my liver was starting with hepatitis and if I didn't stop drinking, I would end up damaging my liver and it would be unable to repair itself.

I attended the SMART meeting on the Monday, I got a lovely warm welcome. This was something I had never seen before. I thought it would be like AA, but it wasn't. This was different it was a group where everyone took part. It dealt with our thoughts, feelings and behaviours and to life a balanced life. It addressed here and now and not the past. I know now why, we cannot change the past, but we can certainly learn from it and this is when I realised, I am not the only one going through this. Other people have gone through it and survived, living happy lives. I found great support in these meetings I was treated with respect (even though I was still drinking). You see when you are alcohol dependant you just can't stop drinking alcohol you need to reduce safely and because alcohol affects the whole nervous system it is dangerous and could kill you.

I had my meeting with my recovery worker, and he referred me to Health and Social Care. The amount I was drinking was over 30 units per day, I was told I would need some kind of medical detox either community based (in the home) or hospital.

Tina my support worker was great, I clicked with her straight away, she didn't judge me. She challenged my thoughts. She painted it how it was. She told me "*We just don't give detox's out from the first meeting*" I told her I was not going to be a revolving door, and I was fed up of my life being controlled by alcohol.

Tina advised me to start reducing my alcohol intake. Hospital beds were few and far between and I wanted my detox at home. When you are drinking over 30 units of vodka per day you have to bring your intake down for a home detox. This suited me fine; I had a goal to work towards. I knew by me admitting I had a problem with alcohol that was my solid foundation for sobriety.

For the next 2 months every other week I would go to Health and Social Care with my drink's diary showing Tina times and dates and circumstances around my drinking cutting down each time I went. We talked about my health both physical and mental health including liver disease, other effects of drinking Wicke Korsakoff's (memory, cognitive behaviour) neuropathy (use of my legs). My relationships with my family and Dan this needed loads of work doing because I had a new best friend in Vodka and everyone else didn't matter. We also discussed my work and whilst I still had a job it was on rocky ground due to the number of sick days I had taken. Finally, my detox because I had to do reduce before I was given one. I wanted a community one (at home). It was good to speak to someone who understood and treat me like a human being.

Tina was the person who suggested therapy after my detox, this was going to be a long road and even though my thoughts of childhood would never go away I would have tools to help me deal with them better and safer.

All through this time I was still attending ladies' SMART meetings, it was rewarding and well worth it, getting "*well done*" from a group of ladies the demographics of the group was an average age of 40 upwards with a couple of younger adults. These ladies knew from their own experience what I was going through. There was emotional support, and it felt good going to Project6. I was treated with respect, an individual and I had hope in succeeding.

I telephoned my team manager to let her know what was happening, I was highly emotional. My employer was very supportive all through this experience, I had the backing from my team manager and the company dealt with addiction as an illness. I had regular telephone as calls just for a quick catch up and no pressure and checking on my progress. I only told of my work colleagues the one who I could trust. She said for me to take my time. It was the first time I was honest with the reason why I was off sick. It was great for it to be out in the open because in the past I had used my anxiety and depression for time off ill when really, I would be drinking all day, every day. I felt the more people knew about me I would receive the best kind of support from everyone.

My home detox was arranged for the 1st July 2019, Dan had booked a full week off work for the detox. I had kept Dan fully informed from the shoplifting experience. He knew when I was going to Health and Social Care and we had discussed him taking time off work. He was proud of me.

I haven't touched a drop of alcohol since.

Barriers

Recovery is never a straight line to progress. You have to overcome obstacles along the way also.

I Was a Barrier to Myself

When battling addiction, it can seem like the road to recovery is blocked at every step. I was the one blocking myself from getting help. Honestly if the security guard had not given me details of Project 6 who knows where I would be.

I had actually gone to Sloan Medical Centre my GP and local drug and alcohol services a few years earlier gone along to get help with my drinking but only went a couple of times as I didn't want to give up. I refused to seek treatment because I didn't believe I had an addiction. It had became a normal part of my day. I thought I could stop on my own when the time was right. I had a denial and unwillingness to give up. I thought that it only affects others not me, I have a job, a house. How wrong I was.

Numbing Myself

I now look at youngsters wanting to get sober and I so wish I had done it sooner. Thinking about my barriers of what stopped me doing that. Vodka helped me forget and to have feelings of safety and warmth. I would go through different scenarios in my head about becoming sober it never happened.

Stigma and Shame

The stigma and shame with being in addiction. Let's face it how society and media portray addicts are the homeless, jobless people not me I had a house, I had a job. I was not an alcoholic, I didn't have a problem with substances. Come on alcohol is legal, it can't possibly be addictive. I was in denial about my problems.

Although our society is starting to recognize addiction is a disease and not a moral or personal failing, remember previously about my feelings "*I need to do 100% in everything.*" I also avoided help for fear of the stigma and worried about losing my job and friends. It was alienating me from my family and loved ones. Every single time my best friend would win Vodka When I think about it I know it was fear.

The best way to reduce the shame and stigma that is often associated with seeking addiction treatment help is through continued education. Only when society and treatment providers alike are on the same page about what it means to have a substance use disorder can the fear of judgment and shame surrounding addiction treatment be dispelled.

Medical Staff

My GP didn't really sign post me to anything, I had gone a different way round to get the help to get sober. I was actually telling them what I had done and who I was engaging with. They did give me my prescription for thiamine and strong Vitamin tablets B12. I had not gone for this it was a sick note I needed and wasn't too sure at this particular time why, now I do.

I never told my mum until I had gone through my detox, she was elderly I didn't want to worry her. There was no relationship with my mum. I went through periods of getting in touch normally asking to borrow money maybe this was some sort of barrier. I would periodically phone my mum; I would invite her at Christmas and like I said tapping for money. I would not visit her at the home I was brought up in, I didn't want it to be part of my recovery. I had got myself into this situation I wanted to do it alone. Also visiting would mean I would need to take a break from my drinking. The bottle always talked me out of it.

I want to be clear on this, all these actions were me and no one else. This was my choice and no one else's. Mum was in her 80's I didn't want her to worry and I probably had shame etc in telling her. If I had have done she would have shown me support and empathy for me. It was best to discuss after the detox.

Stress

Another barrier was coping with stress without substances. One thing I did not realise was the alcohol was feeding into my anxiety and depression. It was making me relax, it was get rid of the awful feeling in my stomach. At this point it was more alcohol withdrawals, and I would take my anxiety medication but it was alcohol which stopped the shakes. It made me forgot about the real issues and I was not being an adult and facing up to anything. I was thinking about what I would be as a person without alcohol. It was giving me confidence, friends life and soul of the party. It was also making me not face up too bills, the care of my home, myself and partner. I was holding onto my job (just about)

Final Reflections

I so wish I had done this earlier; things may have been different. Thinking about it though I had not hit my rock bottom, and the alcohol took me there.

More than once I've thought "*I've got this*!" in my early recovery. "*I thought I knew everything, I didn't I carried on with my recovery attending meetings, speak to peers and finding out things myself. Rent is due every day on keeping sober. I went out to find everything there is to know about recovery and addiction*", I'm still learning. "*I've never thought about dealing with all my issues… I don't need to do any more work on myself*". Yep, that usually happens right before I fall flat on my arse. The growth never stops ever, life is less bumpy and there is always more to know. Being sober is just not enough, I need more than that, if I don't put the work in, then I may stay sober, but it will stop feeling comfortable to me. I would drift back to being discontent and I have to keep looking and reflecting on my behaviour. Behaviours always change before a lapse.

I now know what boundaries are, and my behaviour will show you whether to walk over me, abuse me or hurt me. I can teach people how to treat me, with the boundaries I protect and also by saying what I mean.

I do not waffle on about my recovery journey, I do not need excuses however educating others is what I do best.

Being sober is just not enough, I need more than that, if I don't put the work in, then I may stay sober, but it will stop feeling comfortable to me. I would drift back to being discontent and I have to keep looking and reflecting on my behaviour. Behaviours always change before a lapse.

I do a lot of walking, and I swim now, the benefits of exercising is great, this helps with my emotional well-being, and keeps me fit.

Out of everything, this is the most important one. Seriously, the benefits of exercising on your emotional well-being outweigh almost everything else you can do.

I now have a small circle of quality friends. I surround myself with people I can trust, who can call me out and are there when I need to talk. I always now ask for help no matter how many years

I have been sober. Asking for help is a skill you can never forget.

Going on a journey of sobriety is a courageous decision, it helps me stay connected and accountable. Establish strong support system of family, friends or peers who understand, and support recovery is so important.

Engaging in healthy coping mechanisms, such as exercise, mindfulness practices, and creative outlets, provides a constructive outlet for stress and emotional triggers. Finally, setting new goals, pursuing passions, and fostering a sense of purpose can keep individuals focused and motivated on their sober journey.

I now have a job in alcohol services, I can now pass on my experiences and support to others who are starting their journey. Not only helping and educating to stay sober, it involves helping with self-esteem, confidence and building relationships.

Mum and I did get 4.5 years of sobriety building on our relationship before mum passed away. Unfortunately, she passed away before I got my peer mentor job. I know she would have been so proud.

I would like to end with this:

I dedicate this chapter to mamma bear, shine bright, just like I am. (1937 to 2023).

A Journey of Post Traumatic Growth

Tracey Ford

It has been over 25 years since I was released from a mental institution after being diagnosed with drug-induced psychosis. Back then, I was released with no formal aftercare or signposted to any addiction services.

I often look back to those years and find it hard to recognise the person I used to be. Nowadays I have such a positive, optimistic outlook on life; I work full-time in a managerial position and chair the Sheffield Recovery Community. I have an education (Degree) and am a homeowner. I am financially stable, I have a loving and supportive partner, and I have some amazing friendships, but my life hasn't always been like that.

Learning to become a chameleon

Before I turned to drugs, I'd always somehow felt suffocated by injustice all my young life. I never felt like I fit in. I was raised in an era when adults told us, "*Kids should be seen and not heard.*" I wanted to take woodwork lessons at school but was told I had to take cooking lessons because I was a girl. Mum also encouraged the narrative by dressing me and my sister in what she described as girly clothes. I was never encouraged to express myself, especially not emotions such as anger, which wasn't considered ladylike.

I left school without formal qualifications and a reputation for being a troublemaker. Months after leaving school, I became pregnant and on a crash course into adulthood. I was a child having a child and trying my best to play the role of a dutiful partner and mother - something no naive sixteen-year-old should have to go through, but back then, things were different.

I'd always been an intuitive and sensitive kid. My father was an imposing and intimidating character. You never knew what kind of mood he might be in. The dynamic in the house was forever changing; I was like a chameleon. I'd learned how to read a room and how to adapt from a very young age. It wasn't until Dad left, taking our sofa and TV with him, that the atmosphere lightened, but he was still lurking in the background. As a child, I watched from the sidelines as he raised other women's kids – the rejection was hard.

Numbing My Unhappiness

I'd never considered myself an addict. I'd experimented with cannabis and glue at school but never liked the sensation. But all that changed when I started out using Amphetamines in my early twenties after my then-partner started to sell them. At the time, I was trying to juggle a part-time job; I was fencing stolen goods, including chequebooks. Anything to make my financial ends meet.

Everyone around me was using it; it was the norm, but my use soon became a necessity I couldn't function without it. I'd finally found something that helped me to cope with life on my terms. The drugs helped numb the overpowering feeling of unhappiness; during my highs, I felt invincible; they permitted me to not give a fuck; the only problem was that deep down, I did give a fuck. It wasn't long, say eight months, before my using took me to dark places within myself that I never knew existed. I couldn't see it then, but my family could. I'd lost an incredible amount of weight; I'd become erratic and defensive. I'd never felt so alone and isolated in my life, paranoid that the whole world had turned against me. And I am ashamed to admit that there were times when the option of just ending it all.

Drug-induced Psychosis

It all came to a head shy of my twenty-second birthday when I was admitted into a mental ward and diagnosed with drug-induced psychosis. I will never forget walking through the corridors of the mental institution. All my life, I'd fought hard to try and prove myself, but I'd failed, and the reality of that failure hit me hard. I was an empty shell, void of any emotion,

The staff on the ward were kind. They said everything right, but I didn't trust their words. Words had become meaningless; I had lost my faith in humanity.

As each day passed, I could feel myself getting stronger, but I also knew I was still very fragile and was in no emotional or physical state to face the outside world; in fact, the mere thought of leaving terrified me, but I also knew that I couldn't stay there indefinitely. Weeks passed, and the staff informed me they thought it was well enough to leave, only I didn't feel ready. The hospital ward had become my comfort blanket. It had been the first time I'd felt safe and protected. I didn't confess to them that I didn't feel ready; after all, they were professionals and supposed to know best, so instead, I played along. So, after weeks of being in a bubble, I was thrown back into an environment and into a relationship that had initially caused me harm with no offer of aftercare or support.

It wasn't long before I could feel myself spiralling out of control. I wanted out, but I didn't know how. Or where to go for support. But one day, something inside me snapped. It is hard to explain, but I'd had enough. It was like a lightbulb had been switched on in my head. I finally realised that I would have to make the change if I wanted anything to change. I reasoned that the fear of the unknown couldn't be half as bad as continuing in what I now know was a coercive and controlling relationship.

Cutting Ties From Negative Relationships

At the time, all my life was tied up in what I now know was a coercive and controlling relationship. Intuitively, I knew it wasn't a fair, balanced relationship. Still, I'd persevered and had tried to make it work because I couldn't face the additional shame of being "*just another*" single parent. I'd avoided accessing support, scared of the risk of losing custody or having my kids taken into care.

Starting afresh meant not just leaving my ex, but also turning my back on my old life, including my peer support network. I knew in my gut that if I were to stand any chance of turning my life around, I would also have to reevaluate my friendships after realising that the majority were never really friends, just associates who were engaged in taking drugs and criminality. At times, this felt incredibly isolating and there were many times I would question if I was doing the right thing, the only thing that kept me going was my kids. The stigma of being a single parent weighed heavily, but I had something to prove and I also couldn't bear the thought of losing my kids into social care.

I was initially placed in supported accommodation. The temptation to get back to the life I had walked away from was always there, as was the temptation to take drugs to cope. I shared my concerns with one of the female support staff, one of the few people I felt I could trust. She was outraged when I shared my story and the fact that I had been discharged from the mental health hospital without any form of aftercare and encouraged me to speak to the on-call doctor.

I was hoping that he might give me some prescriptions to help calm my nerves and to help with the cravings. He sat and listened to me for over an hour. Instead of prescribing drugs, he made a referral for a Community Psychiatric Nurse (CPN) to come out to give me some emotional and practical support which I very much needed at the time. Something I now know should have been offered to me as soon as I had been released from the hospital.

Shame

The identity I had once created for myself was shattered into a million pieces. I barely had the emotional capacity to support myself, let alone two kids under the age of seven. It's hard to explain how I got through some of those dark days; I'd ousted myself from my community. I was a mother or two who, in society's eyes, hadn't just failed myself but also failed my kids because of all the unwise choices I had made as a mother. I'd left an aesthetically nice home and swapped it for a maisonette without furniture. I didn't have the financial means to create a home I would have liked to provide for my kids, a home they deserved, but I soon came to realise that I could replace material objects in time, but I couldn't put a price on my mental health. It was me and my girls against the world. They were the only thing that kept me going, as was my CPN worker.

She Saw Something in Me That I Couldn't See in Myself.

She was a great listener; she showed me alternative coping strategies, like journalling, to help me work through my emotions and affirmations, which initially felt strange but somehow started to help. We did a lot of goal setting and how to break each step into achievable actions. Music was another thing that helped distract me from dark thoughts, and my go-to song was "*Search for the Hero Inside Yourself*" by the M People.

Calling the Future "Me" Into Being

My Community Psychiatric Nurse had initially planted and nurtured the seed about going to college. Being a single mum actually worked in my favour regarding returning to education. Back then, there were bursaries for childcare, which was my primary motivation for going in the first place. However, that changed as soon as I walked back into the classroom. At first, I felt stupid and out of place, back at college I was one of a minority of mature students who were there because they'd failed education as kids, but I soon realised that it wasn't me who had failed; it was the system that had failed me.

My experience with education this time was different; instead of being discouraged and written off, I was encouraged. I was doing a sociology course and quickly realised that there was a world outside the bubble I had lived in for the past twenty-three years. One of the course tutors believed that I would make an excellent counsellor because of my past experience, and she applied on my behalf for a bursary to attend a counselling course, which I loved.

On that course, I met the manager of a day rehabilitation programme, who offered me a volunteering position. I was reluctant at first as most of the people on the programme were recovering from heroin addictions and they were mostly men. I was flattered, but I also couldn't see what I had to offer as I had nothing in common with them; I wasn't like them; I'd never touched "*hard*" drugs in my life. Despite my reservations, I decided to give it a go. My role was to help with the day-to-day running of the project. Up until that point, I hadn't talked about my drug use history; It had been something I had tried to brush under the carpet, erase as another bad past episode in my life.

But all that changed after sitting in some of the group therapy sessions. The realisation hit me that I had more in common with the heroin addicts than I thought. I realised it didn't matter what drug I abused because, just like them, my use had been a poor solution to deeper problems in myself. I learned how what we think about ourselves impacts our feelings and, in turn, our actions or reactions. I began to realise that my beliefs about myself weren't necessarily true and that some of my beliefs about myself had been limiting ones, which had been holding me back.

I realised that shame had played a significant role in my life.

I had become an expert in internalising the shame imposed on me by society's moral expectations, and the impact had created a vicious cycle of unhealthy coping strategies. For the first time, I finally felt like I belonged somewhere and had found my tribe. After years of trying to be someone I wasn't, it was time to drop the lie and be around people who weren't afraid to be vulnerable, which permitted me to do the same. My education started to take a different direction as I went inward, and as my thirst for new personal insights grew, so did my passion for helping others.

Final Reflections

All my life, I felt like a contortionist trying to fit in, desperate to feel accepted by anyone. I'd always struggled with friendship and relationships. Now that I know that was because I didn't know what it meant or what it took to have a relationship with myself, I realise that I'd gotten so used to seeking out all the answers from other people because I had no faith in myself.

Since then, I have grabbed every opportunity gifted to me and ran with it, and over time, I developed my sense of self and purpose in life. This also helped me take some accountability. I could have quite easily continued blaming my sham of a life on my ex, my upbringing or the drugs. The reality was that I didn't know any different – that was until someone showed me.

Over the past 27 years, I'd fought hard to be fiercely independent regardless of my gender; also, I had never been offered any gender-specific support before. But once again, that was all about to change when I agreed to participate in a gender-specific research project in 2023. In the initial meeting, which brought together other women in recovery, I shared personal things about myself, usually only reserved for my closest female confidants.

Up until that point, I'd never really had the space to open up and share my vulnerabilities no man could understand, like having to cope with the societal stigma that surrounds women who have failed as mothers. Trying to juggle our own recovery whilst trying to parent and provide for our kid's needs, including their emotional needs. Then there are the unpredictable hormonal struggles we women must navigate and come to terms with.

That meeting served as another stark reminder that I wasn't alone; I'd found a tribe of women who were all on the same page as me; my only regret was that I hadn't met them sooner. Following the research project, I and some other women established Sheffield's first women in the recovery network.

In March of 2024 I was invited to speak at the United Nations to talk about Sheffield women's involvement in the PhD study and to highlight how Mulka's unique approach had inspired women not just to become members of the World Federation Against Drugs (WFAD) International Women's Research network, but also to create their own Sheffield women in Recovery Network.

Working with the ladies also inspired me to create a poem, which was turned into a short film that also won the 2024 National Recovery Street Film Festival called "*Don't Underestimate a Woman in Recovery*". The poem explores a woman's journey through addiction. It delves into feelings of isolation, stigma, and entrapment and how her path changed after connecting with other women in recovery. I have included an excerpt from the poem below:

"Inspired by hope, she tried new and different ways to cope.

She started by surrounding herself with other women who understood her plight, who gave her the courage to continue to fight.

She no longer felt the need to hide, because she'd found her own recovery tribe

With her newfound honesty and open heart, she began to mend ties

that had once been torn apart...
Over time, she's slowly changed the world's view of what a strong, independent woman can do.

And today with her self-esteem and confidence intact, she stands tall.

A reminder to us all that any Woman in Recovery can conquer all."

I no longer like to refer to myself as being someone in recovery; it's just another label, another box for society to put me in. I see myself as a woman who existed in life trying to be someone she wasn't. Someone society expected me to be, well, not anymore. I have learned that if we want things to change externally, we must also be willing to make the necessary internal changes. I'm still on a learning journey, and I am forever learning new things about myself. Writing has profoundly impacted my self-discovery journey; through journalling, I have discovered parts of myself that I never knew existed.

I like to think that by sharing my own lived experience, I can pass on the gifts that were given to me, like hope, encouragement, and faith, to others who do not have any themselves, particularly women. I honestly don't know how I got through those times, But I DO know that had it not been for many individuals who saw something in me that I didn't/couldn't see in myself, I wouldn't be sitting here writing this today.

"It'll be reyt": A Healing Journey in Sheffield

Helena Lovel

So here I am today, a single woman, living my best life. Also known by friends as "*H*". No, its not perfect, I don't live a high luxury lifestyle. Today I live with gratitude, the key that unlocked the door to change everything for me. Living a life I never dreamt I could. At age 50 plus living in one bedroomed flat in supported, recovery accommodation. There's a great staff team who provide support 24/7, looking after around 40 adults, across 3 big houses and 12 flats. So, I live semi independently. I'm responsible to pay my bills and do activities to keep me safe and well. I work for and volunteer with several charities now as a "*person with lived experience*". I feel extremely privileged and grateful for the opportunities.

Some days I'm up and out before 8 am, others I'm in my PJ's all day at home. My recovery has been about me finding my balance. Not doing too much that I'm overwhelmed and break, but also not doing so little that I get bored and depressed. Historically I've done both of those things. So having learnt this I have to be very aware and mindful about what I do now.

My day always starts with gratitude. As I rise from my slumber, I'm grateful to be safe and warm in my own bed. I do this despite being in physical pain. It's a deliberate choice I know I need to make. I have wonderful friendships and relationships with my parents who all help me to be the best version of me. I am doing things now that I never thought I would be able to do back then.

As a woman in recovery, I have experienced many supports and barriers along the way. The rest of this chapter will describe some of what I have experienced in my recovery journey.

Barriers:

When I think about barriers, a fence or guard rail automatically comes to mind. In reality, it's nothing of the sort.

Myself

It has taken a lot of work to get t this point but I have learnt that I was my biggest barrier. I still am my biggest barrier.

I guess I was very much a "*people pleaser*" and could be easily manipulated to do what other people wanted me to do, rather than what I chose. This led to an internal conflict.

I think some people say, "*she fell into the wrong crowd* " or there was "*peer pressure*"

For me I take full ownership of every choice, and the consequences there of. It is by doing this I can also take full ownership and responsibility of my life today.

Yes, I've made A LOT of bad choices, I've also learned from them.

For me, I'd also like now, to give a full and heartfelt sorry, to anyone I ever hurt or who was affected by my behaviours. My intention was never to hurt you, any of you. I simply wanted to escape my own pain.

People's Perceptions

Years ago, I lived in a small town in East Yorkshire, near Bridlington. It was surrounded by farms. Quite a middle-class white place. Many families had lived there years, not mine. It was not a council estate or city centre. It was not a socially deprived area. Both my parents worked, and I was the youngest of 3 daughters. Our home was nice and in one of the nicer areas, my parents had a mortgage. We had good schools and to this day, local independent shops. It is the kind of place where everyone knows each other, and in a time were it's safe for the kids to play out rounders on the street together. Some of my peers have called it posh, to me it's not posh, it's normal.

I come from a respected family, and me even trying drugs would NEVER have been a concern.

This creates another barrier. How other people saw me, versus who I really am.

Lack of Resources and Understanding Locally

The town where I lived, didn't really have any drug or alcohol problems. I remember going to the GP for the first time and asking for help. An idea I had been toying with for months. There was a lot of inner conflict that prevented me from asking for help sooner. Feelings of failure, of feeling weak that if I asked for help, and the denial of the fact that I had a problem that I needed help with. There is also the dread of not knowing how they would respond – would I be judged? Would they understand? I also had to overcome the fact that I had been at this practice all my life and so it was complicated as I knew some of the staff and they knew me. My GP had known me my entire life and my whole family. His wife had been my tutor in college, I knew where they lived!

His reaction was obvious. Although he knew I'd struggled with my mental health, he'd never (not in his wildest imagination) put drugs in the picture. He bolted up and back, wide eyed with shock! He stuttered with shock, offering to help in any way that he could with prescribing services. He even said, "*this has never happened before*". In that moment I felt helpless, lost and alone. If the GP didn't know how to help, then who did? Who would help me now? He rummaged in his drawer for a bit, then pulled out a leaflet. It was for the local service providers that specialise in substance support.

Living in a small rural town meant we had a very limited support services, they were practically non-existent in reality.

There was a tiny room, about the size of a downstairs loo, in a chemist shop in town. A worker from an out-of-town service went for 3 hours one day a week.

So, between 1pm and 4pm on a Tuesday I could go, sit on a seat outside the room, and wait. The worker would look through the window in the door, see me, and invite me in.

Stigma by Professionals

The first reality check with services is that they are extremely slow, slower than a sloth!

I remember pacing outside the chemists before going in, plucking up the courage to be honest.

When I did go in and sit on the chair, I knew the shop staff knew why I was there, not one of them smiled at me or acknowledged my humanity. There'd be a dirty look, aside eye or a smirk. The judgement and shame was very real.

Thankfully the worker showed more empathy and compassion. There was a human conversation here, but lots of paperwork! This is a necessity in all the services, but also a huge barrier for the service user. Whenever you attend a service, you just want to connect with someone and receive the help you need but the amount of paperwork that you need to complete first completely gets in the way of the relationship, and feeling listened to and heard. Anyway, I attended every week for several months, all while waiting for my referral to come through to access the main support services that would then refer me on to relevant services.

I deliberately turned up about 10 minutes before they shut, I didn't want to engage in conversation, I just wanted my clean works and foils and get out.

The worker cottoned on to this, although I didn't realise at the time. They made sure they had what I wanted, but would ask for a mouth swab, or ask a question or 2 in a casual friendly way. I did get to feel comfortable with them.

Stigma From Peers in Rehab

Later in my journey, as a woman in rehab, I also faced some stigma from peers whose substance was different to mine. I received dirty looks, and had derogatory comments made because I was an IV user as opposed to a smoker of heroin. I have also had comments made about me because I have driven whilst under the influence of substances and told that this is worse than those who did drink driving. There were several people whose thinking was that class A substances were far worse than legal alcohol. Some peers were there for both, they and the staff made it very clear this was false. They made it very clear that we were all very vulnerable, unwell people, and only by being aware of this and accepting it, could we allow ourselves to heal.

Ongoing Stigma

Despite lots of amazing stuff and progress, I still see and experience judgement and stigma today. In some places it's very obvious, whether in services, society or within the recovery community. One thing I've found within community recovery circles is how the hierarchy of substances presents itself. Most of the people who use services are there for alcohol. They automatically assume I am too.

In a meeting I'm always honest and say, "*my drug of choice was class A drugs, crack and heroin, and yes I was an intravenous user*". I see the look on their face, as if I'm something they've trodden on. It's as if they think they are better than me for them "*only drinking*". There are a few people who however, really "*Get it*". There is also a hierarchy amongst those who are "*clean*" and not used for a given period and those who may be currently relapsing, even though they once were relapsing too. Addiction is about escapism, recovery is accepting life on life's terms and accepting it. We are all very poorly, vulnerable people. It takes a lot of hard work to maintain sobriety and lead a meaningful life. Who are we to judge?

Mental Health

I've got to be honest here. My thinking at that time during my addiction was very dark. I hated myself, I hated my life. I was extremely poorly. I also didn't see anything wrong in my behaviours or lifestyle. I was on a mission of self-destruction. I'd recently been sectioned for suicidal ideation; I'd tried and failed to end my life several times. I felt an even bigger failure after every attempt because I couldn't even get that right! I wasn't really going for help to stop taking drugs. I was going for clean works and foils, and possibly to get a script. The day they suggested Rehab though, I was very offended! How dare they?! I don't need a rehab I just needed other people to leave me alone and for my existence and pain to end. One day something snapped. I couldn't tell you what or why. I just got sick and tired of being "*sick and tired*".

Turning point

It was November 2015, and this marked a key turning point in my journey. From this point in the chapter, I will now describe some of the themes that have been supports to me in my recovery journey.

Family Support

I ran away. I got in my car and drove, not really knowing where I was going. Part of me wanted to drive into a wall at speed and end it all. But I ended up at my cousin's house and she let me stay. I did a detox there. That was a tough detox. I think I slept for the first week straight. I kept calling services, and in my absence a letter had arrived with my appointment for services support. By this time, I was through the worst, with the physical dependency. I felt like I'd been spat out of hell.

Persistence

I used "*Pester Power*" to phone services 2 - 3 times a week to get an adult social worker. I didn't know if I needed sectioning or rehab.

It took 10 weeks, (which I know now is extremely fast, but at the time it felt like an eternity) for me to find a rehab and secure funding.

I had to do most of this myself. Search online for a rehab, phoning them and arranging a visit.

Thankfully my cousin had a laptop and could support me with this.

It was my responsibility to get there, my anxiety was crippling at this point, I barely left her house. If I did it was only in the car. I couldn't use public transport.

Starting Rehab

Going to rehab was terrifying. I entered this huge house, filled with strangers, and double the amount of men to women. It made me feel very vulnerable as there were people there who were perpetrators of sexual violence towards their female partners and other women. I wasn't sure if I was strong enough to stand up for myself at this point in those mixed gender situations. Also, I wasn't in a place yet to deal with male group dynamics and felt very uncomfortable but had no choice. Inside I was screaming, outside I hid my face in my scarf, and cried daily. The amount of men in the house was very unsettling, some were ok, but some NOT.

There were also some bitchy women, some were loud, some were intimidating others. One lady had it in for me for some reason when I joined rehab. She took an instant disliking to me. I was told by others that she was always saying nasty things about me but never to my face. There was also power dynamics as to who was the prettiest in the house and who got the most male attention which created some interesting power dynamics amongst the women.

It took several weeks for me to loose my scarf and find my voice. I was so very vulnerable and poorly. I didn't want anyone near me, but some peers were very supportive, and the staff were kind. We had shared bedrooms and so we had lots of opportunities for girly bonding, doing one another's hair and sharing toiletries and make up. Staff similarly would be very affirming and encouraging with their comments. At first, I wasn't able to receive their kind comments but over time they taught me to lift my head, roll my shoulders back, make eye contact and say "*thank you*" in response. Having staff with lived experience helped me a lot as they have been where you have been. I remember one staff member come to me after I had said that "*why is it that I am the only smackhead in the village*?" and his response to me the next morning was – "*yeah you are a junkie, just like me*". Everything changed after that. I didn't feel like the outsider, and I was able to identify with him in a completely different way as a result.

There were very strict rules in the rehab, and a strict structure, which I really needed.

With Phoenix Futures, there were several meetings a day, covering lots of subjects. They take dual diagnosis and do in house detox.

They're all shared bedrooms and bathrooms.

Everyday we said our philosophy.

"*We are here because there is no refuge, finally, from ourselves.*
Until we have confronted ourselves in the eyes and hearts of others we are running.
Until we suffer them to share our secrets, we have no safety from them.
Afraid to be known, we can know neither ourselves nor others and will be alone.
Where else but in our common ground can we find such a mirror?

Here, together, we can appear clearly to ourselves not as a giant of our dreams nor a dwarf of our fears, but as a person, part of a whole with a share in its purpose.
In this ground, we can take root and grow, not alone anymore, as in death but alive to ourselves and others."

As I worked through this philosophy and understood its meaning, I got well. We recited it daily, and it was on the wall.

Growing in Personal Recovery Capital

As I progressed through my rehab programme and continually worked on myself, I noticed how I was growing in confidence, becoming more self-aware, I noticed changes in my recovery journal as to how I was feeling each day. My entries changed from, "*today I am feeling scared, or tired or lonely*" to instead "*today I am feeling grateful, or happy, or eager to start the day*". I earned more liberties and privileges. One main one was being trusted to go out alone. Every time I'd been out previously it had been a planned outing with either staff or higher peer support. I was accompanied even if I was going to the GP or for blood tests. I really needed this support to begin with, I couldn't use public transport on my own.

The first time I did go out was to the hairdressers. I honestly can't remember the last time I'd been. As I got to the end of the driveway of the rehab centre, I felt terrified, about being out all alone, unsupervised in the world. I had the responsibility of getting on the bus all by myself and getting to my appointment on time. It was weird and exciting and terrifying. It took a lot of mental self-talk, "I*'m just a woman, going to the hairdressers*", "*it is safe*", "*it is normal*". I'd reached a new level in my healing journey, I felt so proud of myself.

Family

My relationship with my family was a much, much slower process. Most of my family and I don't speak or have any form of relationship. There is some, I'm hoping that at some point we can possibly build bridges. Whilst I also recognise, my previous behaviours have caused them a lot of hurt. I can't turn back the clock and change things, I can simply be my best self today, and hope.

I do now have the best relationship with my parents, and I am very aware (and extremely grateful) that having 2 parents, still married to each other and in reasonably good health is very rare.

The first couple of years were frosty. I was on my healing path with lots of support. They were also recovering from my addiction and the impact on their lives and our extended family.

I stayed at their house for one night at the end of my rehab programme, but it was tense, and on my return to rehab I had a major using dream which really affected me. By simply going to that location, it triggered my muscle memories of using. I cried the entire next day, riddled with guilt, shame, and remorse. I remembered all my old behaviours, the lies, the manipulation, the arguments. It affected every part of me. I decided that day to never do an overnight visit. I needed to be safe and well. I couldn't go back.

Supported Housing

Thankfully, the rehab offered brilliant aftercare support. They had supported housing. It had formerly been called re-entry. A shared house with staff support and we could still go to the rehab for some of their groups, like relapse prevention.

Also, while I lived in rehab, we had the 12-step support group come in alternate Friday nights. The other Friday nights we had SMART recovery people come in.

This gave all residents the opportunity to try other long-term support groups. I'd never done this before; they simply didn't exist in my hometown. But also, my distorted thought process told me, I'd only meet more dealers at a meeting.

Lots of Peer Support

In contrast to my hometown, in Sheffield there is a choice of a variety of meetings, different days, locations, genders. I started going at the end of my rehab programme and continued in supported housing. There was a service in the same part of town. Open 5 days a week!! They had AA, SMART, and other activities and groups. I really took to SMART, the CBT recovery method. With lots of coping tools and strategies for dealing with feelings, and thoughts.

Gender Specific Support

They had a woman only meeting too, which I regularly attended for years. To this day, most of my friends are from those meetings, many of them (like me) also facilitated the meetings too. We just get each other and can relate to each other, and we can talk about topics that we can't if it was a mixed group of men and women. It is a special place that I cherish.

Connection and Community

I think it's as my parents have met my friend's things have really improved. As my parents met my friends, they met "*normal women*" who were also affected with addiction. Women who worked, had families, and some had also been to rehab.

I also think COVID helped a lot too. I think the lockdown helped, as this made us create a communication schedule. I still text them daily and we zoom once a week. We have a much happier and relaxed relationship now.

There have been some uncomfortable conversations over the years, but they have in no way echoed history. I think my parents sleep soundly at night, not having to worry about me, and for that I'm truly grateful.

There's love and laughter shared now, that there never was before. Part of this is me being able to communicate better to them, but also that I have my amazing support network. My friends, staff and peers. These wonderful people, who support me and challenge me to be the best version of myself.

I can be completely open and honest in the circles I move in, in Sheffield. They have only my word on who I was before. I feel completely safe and accepted. I've been fully supported in turning my pain into purpose and celebrating my life. But I've learnt to be very boundaried about who I mix with and what I share.

Discovering My Creative Side

There's also been fun stuff too, fun looks very different these days. I've done painting! Whilst there's probably 10-year-olds that can do a better job, I've come to realise that it's not about that. It's about mindful practice. It's about the people sat with me and the chats we have. It feels really safe, no bodies judging me. Nobody is criticising me or my results.

Growing in My Understanding of My Self, My Strengths, and What Makes Me Unique

Some conversations can be challenging. Learning to listen is really a skill. I struggle with people who talk too fast, or too softly.

I've also learnt about myself, I communicate directly. Yes, I can be blunt, but I never mean any offence. I've also been complimented on how I communicate; I explain things well. Yes, I'm also a bit of a chatterbox, but I can laugh at this trait now and I'm totally ok when someone says, "*H is a chatterbox*". I simply smile, say sorry and shut up. The interesting thing here to note though, I'm also very good at saying nothing. You put me with the wrong people, and I don't speak. I often deliberately sit away from others, alone.

Most people who know me, also know I use my invisible "*hula hoop*" as a boundary. I need my personal space, and I'm very selective over who sits near me and were I sit. This is very deliberate; it is a coping tool for my own well-being. I don't hug everyone, that's not who I am. But those people that I do hug, or who can sit next to me, they are my world. My safety net, my rock. Those people are why I'm here today, alive and well, living my best life.

Voluntary Work, Training, and Employment as a Gateway to Growth, Change, and Empowerment

Since being in Sheffield I've been extremely fortunate in having lots of opportunities. I volunteer with a number of organisations and have been privileged to work on a range of projects. From training to volunteering and paid roles. All of this has been through the recovery community and various service providers. For example, I've been involved with our local service providers and commissioners, something I never imagined could or would ever happen. Recently, we have created a website "*Sheffield Recovery Directory*" (sheffieldrecoverydirectory.co.uk). To bring all the services together, to promote and empower with choice our new service users. This will hopefully go a long way to make a city a Recovery Inclusive City, a status we strive to achieve.

Joining Changing Futures provided by South Yorkshire Housing Association (SYHA) in 2022 was a complete game changer. They are specifically funded to look at 5 areas of multiple disadvantage: Addiction/ recovery; Mental Health;

Domestic Abuse; Criminal justice system involvement; Homelessness. I have lived experience of the first 3. This has been funded by a special government grant to support adults with multi disadvantage. This role has been amazing, I've had loads of really good learning opportunities here. Many of them have really had a positive impact on my life, it's built my confidence and helped me expand my comfort zone. They are an amazing staff team, and brilliant peers. I've made some brilliant connections here and I am really grateful to all of them. It could be that I do an online meeting, or maybe go to the office for a workshop. I can honestly say, I've done things I never thought I could do!

I've been able to be involved in lots of work streams as part of the coproduction team. We've even coproduced the coproduction training that is being rolled out in Sheffield with all services. None of this is happening in my old hometown. As I've evolved personally, and with support, the roles I've been invited to take part in have also expanded. I'm now part of the National Expert Citizens Group. They are a team of lived experience adults from around the country who are lottery and government funded. We get questions sent from Whitehall about services and systems. We often look at what is working, what isn't working, and how it can be improved.

Being part of this team is very special and important to me. I've made friends with others around the country and together we've learnt so much. Many of our meetings are online, but there's some in person too. Being part of this team has really helped me gain confidence and stretch my comfort zone. I've even travelled on public transport on my own, something I couldn't do at the start.

Another role I do is with the Amy Winehouse Foundation. Going into schools and speaking with youngsters about my lived experience. A role I'm very grateful for and feel very passionately about.

I'm also an Expert by Experience (EBE) with Rethink, the mental health charity. We do a variety of coproduced roles to support the local services and service users. I can only do all these roles because I'm living in recovery in Sheffield. I've got an amazing support network of friends, staff and peers.

Self-Care Rhythms and Routines

I very deliberately have to carefully balance my time and lifestyle. I've learnt the hard way. Do enough to keep me occupied, without becoming overwhelmed. My self-care must be balanced constantly. I have multiple diagnosis for mental and physical health. Keeping to a certain routine is essential: I go swimming, I practice mindfulness. I eat well, and make sure I have fun! But the one thing, that I have now, which I never had before is definitely "*an attitude of gratitude.*" As I open my eyes each day, I'm grateful. It turns everything around for me constantly. No, my life isn't perfect, but it's far better than it once was, and I am truly grateful.

Reflections

Something brilliant happened in September 2024. As usual Sheffield had our annual recovery awareness and celebrations. An entire month dedicated globally to recovery. In Sheffield we had a variety of events, beginning with a walk through the city, including all services and commissioners. A very busy month of activities and events.

My favourite part was the Friday 27th. A long but amazing day, Starting with the Recovery Street Film Festival Awards. My SWIPE sisters had made a film, "*Never Underestimate A Woman In Recovery*". This is a newly formed women's group in Sheffield. I don't think any of us had previously considered how our gender had impacted our recovery journey. We had been notified we were shortlisted and got tickets to the award ceremony at The Showroom Cinema. It was a really high energy day. Lots of people from across the country had come to Sheffield, to celebrate. Including last year's winners, "*Detox Factor*". Everyone was so excited and happy. We watched all the films, then Detox Factor performed. We all got up and danced, such a brilliant atmosphere. All of us celebrating recovery, dancing, singing and waving our purple flags. It was amazing, the best natural high I've had, living free of substances. Then came the awards. There were some brilliant, powerful, inspiring stories. Yet ours was awarded 1st place! I just remember hearing my bestie squealing with delight as we erupted with cheers and went to the front. I was overwhelmed with pride and joy. Bursting with happiness and gratitude. Being there, in that moment, with people I love. Those that keep me safe and well. It was a real buzz! The best feeling ever. I had to wipe my eyes as I soaked in the feelings.

Following this, we then had the closing ceremony at the Town Hall. Lots of important people from all over the city, including the Mayor. I entered the room, still on a natural high with our 1st place Trophy, firmly in my grip. It was brilliant!! Lots of friends congratulating us. Seeing peers I'd not seen for years! A bit of a reunion. One of my former peers had a stall for the hep c trust. He showed me pics of his wife and son, I hadn't seen them for 5 years. Then I bumped into D, he was a worker at the rehab, I'd met him on the first day I got here. We smiled as we greeted with a hug, me with my trophy that I proudly showed off. He was so happy for us, congratulating our win. *"I bet you never thought that night in the annex, when you popped your head round the door to meet me, we'd be stood here today", "O my word! No"* he replied, *"how long ago was that? It must be 10 years," "almost"* I replied. *"It's 9 years."* 9 years, I still can't quite believe it myself. I came to Sheffield thinking, I'd do 6 months in rehab, then go home. Obviously, the universe had other plans!

Women Do Recover

Aliyah Knight

After many years of suffering with poor mental health, being in and out of secure inpatient institutions, being passed from pillar to post with different professional health care services after trying to end my life, I am here today, and I want to share my story with you to show that there really is light at the end of the tunnel. I am living proof of this. You just need to keep on going…

My Life is Better Than I Could Ever Have Imagined

I never thought in a million years that life could be this wonderful. I never knew what it felt like to be at peace and content until now. I never thought I'd be able to walk around in my own community with my head held high. I never thought I'd be able to trust someone again, love someone again or feel safe with someone again. I never ever knew what true happiness felt like. The biggest lesson I have learnt in life is that "*Growth Starts With Change, and Change Starts With You*". The life I live now, is by far better than one I could have ever imagined. I have a job that makes me so happy, it gives me a sense of purpose every day. I'm extremely lucky to be able to work in an environment where it's safe to share my story and lived experience with the vulnerable people that I support because they say I inspire them. Until I found recovery, I was one of these people. Struggling to battle everyday life and self-medicating just to do so. However, now I wake up every morning without fail and I automatically connect with my inner self through prayer and meditation. I spend time with my family and friends that are encouraging, supportive and are invested in seeing me thrive. I have met a man that is kind, loving and gentle who forever brings the best out in me. I am always looking for opportunities to connect with others and contribute to the community and the environment around me. I live in a house that finally feels like a home. I eat healthy, sleep well, connect with nature at any given opportunity, I am addicted to going to the gym and Pilates. I am forever practising compassion for myself, I can finally say, I LOVE ME, I love who I am, I'm proud of who I am, and every scar I have tells a story. A story that is able to give another suffering individual hope, strength, and courage that things do get better. My full outlook on life has changed, I no longer sit in self-pity when something bad happens to me, instead I stop and think what is this lesson teaching me, what can I learn from this situation. Since doing so, I've been able to change my pain into power.

I'm going to share my story, I'm sharing my story for YOU, I'm sharing my story to prove that even when being called a "*Psychopath*" or a "*little victim*" or a "*fruit loop*" or a "*druggie*" those words will never define me. They will never define YOU.

I'm doing this for every person out there who is enduring abuse, or unable to cope with their poor mental health or who is killing themselves due to their drug and alcohol addiction thinking that there is no way out. Well guess what? There is a way out, RECOVERY is possible.

I'm writing this feeling truly grateful that I had a lucky escape, while knowing for some it's a little too late…

This is MY story, and my story will not be silenced!

My Trauma Led Me Into Addiction

I didn't think justice could ever be served, nor closure ever be gained. Trauma is not erasable, and time is not refundable. You can't change the past, but you can change your future.

From age 14 to 21, I was in a domestic violent relationship that robbed me of my innocence. It robbed me from my teenage and adolescence years. It robbed me of my life. I was physically, mentally and emotionally abused in the most unimaginable, disgusting ways. He abused me in my sleep and while I was awake. Day in and day out. Beaten so bad, I miscarried and that's a loss I will forever pine for. However, he was like a drug to me, I became addicted to his vile behaviours and actions. So blinded by his "*love*" that I thought what was happening to me was normal, it was okay. So, I accepted it because I felt worthless. He left me feeling isolated, abandoned, empty and fragile. I didn't know who I was anymore, I didn't have any interests or hobbies, I didn't know anything anymore I was completely lost and broken for a very long time. He silenced me for so many years, taking away all my freedom and my voice. I became like an empty shell that was scared of her own shadow, until I left, and I never looked back.

That version of myself, I don't think I will ever stop grieving for. I've just learnt to live with it and accept it for what it was, because it shaped me to who I am today. A woman that has a mind and body that no one could ever destroy again.

Taking every bit of strength, I didn't know I had. I came forward and spoke out. I told my parents what was happening behind closed doors. I did this because I believed there was no other way out. I continuously feared for my life. How can someone I love, someone I share my mind, body and soul with hurt me in this way? How? I failed to understand that my nervous system would always choose familiar chaos over unfamiliar peace until I chose to heal and chose differently.

Barriers in My Recovery Journey

I faced many different barriers that prevented me from finding recovery. The first one being the fear of taking that first step and admitting that I needed help because I couldn't do it on my own. I tried so many times and failed. I had a fear of being "*labelled*" and seen differently for being properly diagnosed with mental health conditions. I was scared I would be penalised for being a person with Bipolar and PTSD, that it would affect my future career pathway if I was knocked back from certain job roles for being seen as "*not fit* " for the role. Ultimately, the fear of being seen as less than and not capable of anything. I had a fear of being seen as a "*victim*" if I disclosed my DV relationship and I assumed that people would see me as a weak individual.

Family and Cultural Shame

Also, my gender, age and culture were a big barrier in my recovery as I'm a young female who is mixed-race and I was brought up being taught that drugs, alcohol and sex before marriage were haram in my Islamic culture. Therefore, it is a big sin. So, I had a big fear of being rejected by my family and disowned for bringing "*shame*" on them. Additionally, because of my age, I was at risk of external factors. These were a massive barrier in my recovery because I was more likely to be involved in environments where drugs and alcohol were used. It was seen as a normal "*fun*" thing to do when going out on the weekend to parties with my social group. There was a lot of peer pressure to try different drugs also.

Feelings of Hopelessness

There were many difficult obstacles that I faced along my journey to recovery where I honestly believed "*this is the end of me, I want out of this life*". I had no hope whatsoever that things could get better, because no matter how hard I tried to deal with what was going on inside my head, the voices inside me took over my full life. They made me feel numb, empty and completely broken. I was honestly so powerless over these emotions. So, in order to cope with these negative feelings and emotions, I started taking drugs. Whenever I was under the influence or intoxicated, I would feel a sense of ease and comfort for a very short while. They would help me think and feel less. I was able to block out my trauma. They would give me false confidence and pleasure, helping me feel like I finally fit in and gave me a sense of importance/belonging. So, before I knew it. I became dependent on substances and my life became rapidly unmanageable. I said and done things I always said I never would just to feed my addiction. I was so selfish, insecure and dishonest. I lost my job, so I was in debt up to my eyeballs. I lost my family and friends because they were ashamed of me and the person I had become. I lost everything. I knew I needed help, but I was helpless because no one was able to understand me.

Lack of Support From Professionals

I reached out for professional help because I was having severe suicidal thoughts, and I was self-harming a lot. When I was having a medical assessment from my GP, I was left feeling worthless because of her response to what I was trying to explain to her. She looked right through me as if I was a piece of shit on the bottom of her shoe and said "*If you don't know how to explain what you feel like then I can't help you. I can't read minds. I'm not a genius*". As you can imagine, this made me feel as if what I was feeling wasn't normal, I felt like I was the only person in the world feeling that way and that I wasn't "*normal*". I remember feeling like I just wanted to scream and shout because no one understood me. I felt so ashamed and humiliated. I wasn't able to cope with feeling how

I did, and professionals did not help me. The only thing that would help me escape from reality was smoking cannabis. So, I did this for many years. From the excessive amount of substances I took, I caused myself to have drug-induced psychosis and I was put on a section 2 in a secure inpatient mental health hospital. In and out of services for over a year, I finally became diagnosed with multiple mental health issues and was referred into ParkSide secondary care where I was clinically medicated. I was allocated a CPN who signposted me to bereavement counselling and referred me to my Sister's Place so that I was able to heal from all my past trauma. I was given tools that would help me manage my triggers and there was a safety plan made for me if I ever found myself in crisis again.

Things That Helped Me in My Recovery

I learnt that healing is an art. It takes time, it takes practice, and it takes love. I learnt that recovery is about progression, not perfection.

Creating Daily Rituals and Routines

Sleep therapy and meditation helped me a lot in my recovery because when I had a healthy sleeping pattern, I felt more energetic, and my overall mood increased so I felt more positive and started to make small changes to my life. One thing was I started going on walks more often, I started the gym and met some new friends. I also set myself small goals that were achievable, so I felt a sense of purpose.

12-Step

The most important thing that helped me in my recovery journey is completing the 12-step programme with my sponsor and attending weekly fellowship meetings. The programme changed my life in so many ways. It gave me the ability to learn and understand my defects of character, so I was able to work on them and become a better person. It encouraged me to make amends with all the people that I had wronged and caused harm to while in active addiction, so I formed stronger connections with my family and friends. It enabled me to forgive myself for all the things I accepted in the past, all the bad choices and mistakes that I made so I no longer feel ashamed or guilty. I'm now able to accept things and people for what they are. CA has also allowed me to meet people that are similar to me, that understand me and can relate to me. Most importantly, all thanks to completing my steps, I'm very spiritual and believe in a power greater than myself. I'm so grateful that I no longer feel the urge to use any mind-altering substances.

Working in a Lived Experience Recovery Organisation

My job also plays a massive role in my recovery journey because it's the first organisation that I've worked for in my life where you are inspired to be free and to be who you really are. As a lived experience organisation, I am able to share my story with the people I support to encourage them that recovery is possible.

My story helped me to realise that in every case, pain had been the price of admission into a new life, but this admission price had purchased more than I ever expected. It brought me a measure of humanity, which I soon discovered to be a healer of pain. I began to fear pain less, and desire humility more than ever.

A Journey of Hope

Jennifer Bryson

My name is Jennifer, I am a person in long-term recovery having just celebrated 10 years of abstinence from alcohol and all other drugs. Wow, that still makes me emotional to write that or say it out loud! Life looks very different to how it did just over 10 years ago and I am so immensely proud of myself and grateful for the support I have received along the way. Recovery isn't always easy but it is SOOOO worth it.

Life Today

Today life is busy, I have a job where I get to work in a LERO (Lived Experience Recovery Organisation). I actually get to be a leader in a LERO which still amazes me to this day. I have my children back in my life which is equal amounts of immense pleasure and pure exhaustion which I wouldn't change for the world. I get to have one of my children live with me full time and the other, lives between myself and his father. I have an amazing family around me, a fantastic supportive partner and some amazing lifelong friends. I have people in my life who I can connect with in a way which wasn't even in my awareness 10 years ago, let alone something I thought possible.

I try to keep myself fit and healthy although this fluctuates on many levels for many reasons but I do my best on any given day to make good life choices. I enjoy reading, connecting with friends, love films and books and my favourite pastime is baking. I can spend hours making a mess and baking multiple things at once and you will never see me happier than when I'm in the middle of a messy kitchen covered in flour. I love meditation and mindfulness and this is still a huge part of my life and Recovery, as are the 12-steps and SMART Recovery and the things they have taught me along the way.

Life is good! Not always easy but good, great even!! Fantastic on some given days. Even when life doesn't feel so great, it's so much better than the life I used to lead.

My Recovery Journey

So, I hear you ask, how did I achieve this life and how did I achieve 10 years substance free? It started by being made aware of what services were available to me. I had accessed services in the past and they always asked me what I wanted, I used to say that I wanted to be a social drinker and just wanted to stop needing to drink every day. They would ask what support I wanted, and I would shrug my shoulders so they would give me a drinks diary and ask me to fill it in and bring it back in 2 weeks for my next appointment. At this time, no one actually told me what was on offer and what I could access so I thought that 1 appointment every 2 weeks was all that I could have.

I had attended my GP surgery numerous times for help, my parents kept telling me that if I just went there and admitted I had a problem then there would be loads of help for me however time after time, I went to appointments, asked for help and was told, there was no help for people like me, that people didn't get sectioned who had an alcohol problem, that you can only go to rehab if you had the money to pay for it, which I didn't and so I would leave deflated and think that this was my lot in life and there was no hope of becoming better.

I feel like I need to say, some of the people I worked with along the way were lovely people and I could tell they cared but I just felt like they didn't have a clue and weren't able to help me with any kind of support that I actually needed, even though at the time, I'm not sure even I knew what I needed.

Arrested for Drink Driving

A few months down the line and I was arrested for driving whilst under the influence of alcohol for the second time. A support service that my family were working with asked to come and visit me, and within the hour they were at my door. I was in withdrawal and didn't have the money to buy anymore alcohol and I actually didn't want to drink anymore. They took me straight to the Doctors and demanded I was given medication to stop the withdrawal and then over the next few weeks she explained what was available. She came to court with me and made sure I got the right worker to suit my needs within a service. I started to fully see what was available and what I could access.

The lady who originally came to see me, where my journey started to take a different direction for the first time, treated me like a human, she took charge but explained things to me, gave me choice and a full list of options. She treated me with kindness and respect and it came at a time when I was open to the thought of change which was the catalyst in my recovery journey.

Community Support

I wanted rehab but there was a wait so I started to access a community of people who were just like me, a few weeks sober/clean up to a few years sober/clean. I was scared of the world and everyone in it so I would sit in the corner of the room and listen and take in everything going on around me, I loved being there and it felt like home. Even though I was unable to fully engage at the beginning because of my own fear and anxiety, the service and everyone accessing the service alongside me, gave me space and time. They gently worked with me and I started to open up and get more involved. There were activities every day and I got involved in things like Reiki, yoga, cooking, IT, SMART recovery, women's group, arts and crafts and lots, lots more. It was a place where I could be open about my past, my feelings and start to become my true self. I wasn't judged, people had generally lived similar lives so had done some of the things I was utterly ashamed of and yet I saw them happy, healthy and living their lives. No matter what people had done in their past, we were all accepted here. I was safe. After years of alcohol abuse, domestic violent relationships, mental health issues and trauma after trauma, I had found people and a place where I felt safe, where I saw hope of becoming better, hope that people can go on to lead normal lives even with pasts like mine. The openness to talk about emotions, to hear that people felt just like me and learning how to cope with emotions and not allowing emotions to dictate behaviours was a huge part of my recovery journey.

The Support of a Recovery Champion

The support I received was second to none in this service, my finances were in a mess and a worker helped me apply for grants so that I could go bankrupt, and she helped me all the way through this process. I know she was told halfway through the process that she shouldn't be helping me in this way and was not allowed to do so. However, she continued because she had already agreed to help me with this, and this was invaluable in my journey. The debts and fears and anxieties around people coming to my door for money. The fact I couldn't even afford to offer each creditor £1 a month weighed heavy on my mind and so did the thoughts of me being stupid for finding myself in this place.

Mental Health

My mental health was on the floor when I started to access service. I had attempted suicide numerous times whilst still in active addiction and self-harmed daily. One of the main problems I had in getting support was that alcohol teams didn't want to work with me because my mental health was too bad. However, on the opposite side, mental health teams didn't want to work with me because they said I was drinking too much!! Mental health support led me to receive numerous diagnoses such as undiagnosed post-natal depression, severe depression and anxiety, insomnia and psychosis.

Eventually, I was allocated a CPN who worked with me whilst I was still drinking but carried on for a period of time while I became sober. He was great, he was empathetic and non-judgemental, he didn't make me feel ashamed or guilty if I turned up and had had a drink that day, he worked with me regardless of how I attended and gave me time and held a safe space for me. I felt heard and valued at these sessions, I was also given hope that how I currently was, was not how I had to stay forever, I knew it was going to be a journey, and I was struggling to see the possibility of becoming better however it was the first time there was a glimmer of hope. I remember one things that he taught me which was about your brain being unable to be in a cognitive state and an emotional state at once therefore counting backwards from 1000 in different numbers or counting numerous things and keeping lists in my head, would stop the overwhelming fear and emotion to allow me to get to where I needed to be and this really worked and helped, I had struggled to get out of the house, I had struggled to walk down the street or get public transport without having a panic/anxiety attack and this tool helped me no end, especially in the first few years of recovery however he helped me with so much more, self harming, insomnia, anxiety, depression. I still use some of those tools to this day when I feel anxiety creep in because I may be sober however that doesn't mean life is rosy or perfect in anyway. I just have different ways of coping with life today rather than reaching for a bottle.

Family Life

My family life and relationships had taken a real beating whilst I was in active addiction. I had stolen from my family and treated my loved ones in a way which I am not proud of. My children's father got a residency order so that the children would live with him and I would have supervised contact with them through my family members. Social services came in and out of our lives for many years which is a really scary process to be involved in, every time we got a new social worker, I would need to go through everything from the start and explain all of my flaws, although I was proud of the progress I was making, I was still ultimately ashamed of where I had come from and retelling my story over and over never became any easier. Having multi-disciplinary team meetings with everyone around the table staring at me, having to explain every part of my life to strangers and prove the progress I was making was difficult, everyone had an opinion on my life, what I should do and how I should live and how I should deal with my children. With one of my children having additional needs, this further impacted the complexity of our situation and again everyone had an opinion. I never felt good enough and every meeting came with fear and anxiety in the weeks leading up to it. I was judged and stigmatised and looking back, there was a clear lack of understanding around addiction although I didn't see it at the time, comments like I should go and have a hot toddy when I had a cold etc were not really very appropriate however I was so focused on getting my children back in my life that they could have said anything or told me to do anything and I would have done it. I absolutely felt judged and stigmatised by the people around the table every time I had to go to yet another meeting and this further impacted the way I already felt about myself, not good enough, a terrible mother, a terrible human being in general. It was a hard process and every day at times felt like a battle. I guess, I didn't consider this at the time however due to me being purely ashamed of myself, I felt like I deserved the judgement and the shame from myself and others. From memory, I have had at least 10 different social workers in and out of my family's life for the best part of 12 years, some were nice people and wanted to help but didn't always get things right, others were not very nice people and my last social worker was absolutely fantastic, she listened to me, the children and their father, she was direct but caring, she was able to see things from all perspectives and give opinions without judgement, she cared and it seemed like she really wanted the best for me and my family. Getting things back on track was not easy especially in the early days because I didn't feel like I deserved forgiveness or love from anyone. Finding people like me is what helped me keep going, each of us supporting one another to carry onto another day.

12-Step Fellowship

The help and support I received from my workers at the community centre was also invaluable and one of them took me to my first 12-step fellowship meeting one day when he asked me how I was doing at the right time in the right place and I fell to my knees and told him that I was struggling to just not drink every single day, I wanted to drink, it consumed my thoughts and I hated the person I was, he told me that I needed a meeting and took me the following day. Fellowship meetings were fantastic in my recovery, although I was still nervous, anxiety ridden and shy, I attended and listened. It took me until I was 9 months sober to be able to say "*my name is Jen and I am an addict*" but the power in the rooms is phenomenal.

Volunteering & Employment

I was told that I would need to stop going to the service after I reached a certain point of sobriety, so I decided to become a volunteer. This way, I could continue going for as long as I wanted. I started by volunteering in a breakfast club which was great fun and I worked alongside some fantastic people who helped me more than they will ever know. People showed me love, care and compassion, they reassured me that I was not a bad person and that I had lost my way but helped me believe I could find a way back from the depths of despair, they helped me find my passion and talents, believe that I was worth something, they held hope and love for me when I had none and they believed in me until I could believe in myself. Then I went onto complete the ambassador programme to support my learning in how to work in the field which was only a dream at this point, and I never thought it would actually become a reality but today I write this as a leader in a LERO. Having done multiple jobs within the field, each and every one, I have loved for different reasons. Being a volunteer and feeling like I had found my tribe and taking slow steps at taking on more responsibility like taking the attendance lists and helping support the delivery of groups which massively helped my confidence and self-esteem. When I was programme support and helping support people who wanted to get into rehab, I really found that I was good at something, meeting people where they were without judgement, supporting them to get to appointments and attend what they needed to in order to get into rehab, accompanying them to appointments and meetings was an amazing role and really helped me see the potential in myself. As a rehab coach, this felt really responsible, like holding someone's recovery in your own hands however the work I did with people as a rehab coach helped me to reflect on my own journey and work on parts of me that I had not considered before, it strengthened my recovery and supported me to further grow and believe that I could do and be more than I had ever dreamed of before.

When I was asked if I would consider applying for a managers role, I said "*no thank you*", I had no desire to be a manager however what my previous experience showed me was that sometimes people can see things in you that you don't necessarily see in yourself so with a little gentle persuasion, I stepped into a community managers role and this was so much fun, it was hard work but really rewarding, another step to show me that I was capable of so much more than I had ever thought possible, each role after this was more learning and growing and evidence that I was capable, that I was good at something and the support I have received on my journey has been phenomenal, I haven't always gotten things right and here, that is ok, we look at mistakes as learning events and this has provided a safe space for me to be able to learn, grow and explore, to build my confidence and learn how to get things right (not all of the time, mistakes still happen, that's normal and that's still ok). I have met some amazing people along the way who have helped, supported and guided me, some I now have the privilege to call my friends. My job and career path has provided much needed help, learning, guidance, direction, passion and motivation in my life in the last 10 years, and I will be forever grateful to those who came before me that have showed me the way and what was possible. I am now in a role which I am finding my way through, its new and I am not 100% sure what it is going to look like but I know with the support and guidance, I will be ok, I will do ok and I know that I will always give 100% and always do the best for the people we support.

Reflections

My journey has been empowering, fulfilling, beautiful, scary, difficult, fun and sometimes all of these things at the same time. I have faced lots of adversity along the way, sometimes feeling like every day is a fight but I am here. It has made me stronger and made me the person that I am today.

Being a person who has been in multiple DV relationships and getting used to being around men, having a male worker at times and having male colleagues has been difficult. In the beginning, I struggled being around men until some amazing males in my life showed me that men are not all like the males, I experienced prior to being in recovery. This took time and lots of it, some fantastic humans in my life to show me that there are some good people in the world and restoring my faith in the human race.

Having experienced multiple years of social worker involvement and feeling like the worst person and mother in the world, this has been difficult, and I am not sure that guilt and shame will ever stop being sparked at different times and in different situations however love, care and compassion, human to human interaction rather than the power imbalanced dictatorial approach was found and won in the end. I am so happy to say that the relationships I have built with my children in the last 10 years is beautiful and we have the most amazing relationship today.

Looking back on my journey, each hurdle I have overcome has had 1 thing in common and that is people. Non-judgement, beautiful souls who have helped me along the way, showing love, care, compassion and empathy for me, listening to me vent and cry when I have needed it and in turn doing that for others when they have needed it. Connection has been my key to unlocking the most powerful journey a human could go through.

I am not proud of some of the things I have done in my past however I do embrace those times and they empower me and motivate me to be the best version of myself that I can be on a daily basis.

I am forever grateful for the life I live today.

Courage to Heal

Sarah Schonewald

This Is Me

I wake up each morning being grateful for all the amazing things I have in my life right now. Not each day is perfect but each day I wake up want to be a better version of myself than I was the day before. I have always wanted big things in life, a career, a perfect house, family, partner, the idyllic fairy tale just like any young woman growing up. I now know that in the real-world fairy tales don't exist because life throws things at us that change our path in life not even realising that is happening.

A Roller Coaster of a Life

Life has been one long, tough, chaotic rollercoaster with many up and downs, many highs and lows. Plenty of my kinda highs unfortunately, mostly the ones I could sniff up my nose or smoke on a crack pipe to numb the pain of the life I was trapped and being suffocated in.

I am Sarah, the new reborn me who wakes up each day feeling blessed to be able to hear the birds singing and feel the cold fresh wind on my skin. At the age of 39 I have finally found my inner peace and living the best life I ever had. Master's student !! yep that's me, she made it! The girl who lost her children, was homeless with nothing but the clothes on her back, doors closed on her and now on my way to my goal of my PHD. I grew up in a dysfunctional family, mam drank a lot, and my dad lived next door just to make things even more fucked up. There were always arguments, I never had a bad childhood, I was loved by both parents but If social services existed in those days child protection wouldn't have had a look in.

The Wrong Crowd and Domestic Violence

From an early age I was always attracted to the wrong crowd. Bad lads older than myself, jailbirds which looking back now they lead me down the path of destruction. At 15 I was in an incredibly controlling domestic violent relationship with a man a lot older than myself. That relationship led to a repetitive pattern of domestic violence relationships all the way through my twenties which consisted of me being battered daily, living a life of misery and being introduced to class A drugs. For all I lived in the madness I always had ambitions and goal that I really tried my hardest to pursue but because of his drug addiction and the domestic violence it was impossible. I started at Northumbria University on a mental health nursing degree and gave it my best shot, but life was too hard, and I couldn't do it. I beat myself up so much and felt a failure for not finishing what I had started, and I began to use substances to cope with everything that was going on around me. I was petrified to go home because I would be accused of madness, affairs etc. and so the drink would help me build my courage to go in and face what was coming to me that night. It would make me fearless, or the hidings would hurt less but either way I was coming off worse.

Becoming a Mother

He took advantage of me massively and I became pregnant at 16 completely hypnotised by his narcissistic ways. Becoming pregnant wasn't ideal, but I was always mature for my age, and I thought I knew it all. The pregnancy had complications from the start but all I knew was I wanted this baby so much and I wasn't going to give up it. I went into early labour at 32 weeks and my baby boy was born, the scariest time of my life. I listened to all the babies crying and mine didn't. He was the most beautiful thing I had ever saw in my life, I sat by his bed side for 9 weeks until the hospital gave up and I held him in my arms while he fought for breath. This was mind blowing and surreal, I had no support for his loss from family or anyone else. I was a young woman battling the loss of her baby whilst living a life of violent hidings and fear. Years later, I had a young daughter and a young son who I loved more than life, I did my best every day to be a great mum and keep them safe.

My children were always my life but looking back now I can see that I didn't enjoy motherhood or my oldest two kids when they were babies because it was always overshadowed by the men who I let control my life. Children's services became involved when my partner at the time self-referred to treatment services for his heroin addiction. As soon as they became involved, I felt as judged as he was when I didn't use drugs. I was clueless about the system and instantly I was petrified, I always felt like they were out to get us because I didn't understand, and no one was willing to explain. After months of persecution, judgement and fear I experimented with crack cocaine as a way of coping, and they took my children which broke me. They gave me a reason to no longer fight or want to live.

My life spiralled out of control and became a constant battle, trying to juggle domestic violence, social services, having to prove myself as a mother constantly mentally drained me. The pressure was too much, and it pushed me further into using substances, people say how can that be? It was the catalyst of my self-destruction but also the reason that I was losing everything around me. I couldn't see for the heartache I was feeling inside, I just wanted it to go away. When you lose your children even if its for a short period of time it feels like some one rips you heart out. It's a pain that you cannot describe. Worse than grief. You don't want to wake up in a morning and when you do the first thing you think about is how quick can I numb this unbearable pain because the loss eats you away like a cancer. I punished myself mentally and physically for the weak mother I was and for not being able to be the person everyone expected me to be, and I had nothing left to give. I was at my lowest, rock bottom with just the clothes on my back.

My Turning Point

I remember the day I decided that I couldn't live this way anymore. It was New Year's Eve, and I was in my mother's house waiting to see in 2018. I remember it hit twelve and I heard all the celebrations and fireworks. I sat in my mother back bedroom on my own with two black eyes homeless and I cried a river. I couldn't stop crying and I couldn't believe how my life had turned out. I drank wine like there was no tomorrow and I felt so alone and empty thinking what next? That was a key changing moment in my life, and I told myself that I was going to fight for everything I loved, and I deserved more in life.

It was hard, I didn't know where to start. Most of the time ended up on a bender because me and my mother didn't get on. She would get drunk; call me names and I would find any place to just to get out the way. My priority was finding a place to live, and I couldn't do that without money. I have had good jobs in the past so luckily it didn't take me long to find employment and I worked for a popular call centre and with the first month's wage I used it as a deposit for a house not far away from my children. I was still using though, spending my wages sitting in a crack house then waking up traumatised because I was skint for the next month. For all I was taking small steps forward there was still a void in my life that drink and drugs filled. Soon as the second bottle of wine went down it was like a switch went on in my brain. I craved lines at first then the more drunk I got, the more I wanted a bigger high. I never used heroin, and I thought that put me into a different class. I look back now, and I was no different. Only difference was I didn't steal for my fix, I worked or manipulated situations to get it.

Looking for Help

This went on for months, I couldn't do it completely on my own and what reason did I have to really? I self-referred to Wear Recovery and was given a key worker who hadn't misused substances in the past, a lovely bloke but he didn't have a clue. I used to try and explain how I felt but what would he know, he was not a woman and will never understand the bond between a mother and her children. He suggested to join one of their groups but never explained what I would get out of it so I didn't really pay much interest.

The first group I attended was a mixed recovery meeting and I remember feeling like I didn't belong there. I felt like I didn't want to talk about me or my life in front of a room full of strangers, I was ashamed. I always said I will never lose my kids and end up a crack head as some would say, but I did. It can happen to anyone in a heartbeat. I attended I think about 6 -8 groups, and I met women in the same boat as me which was comforting. If it hadn't been for her I probably would have fucked it off straight away.

Losing My Job

I was never substance free the whole time I accessed that service, and I believe that was because after the group it was "*see ya later*". I lost my job in the call centre because I had been on an all-night session on coke and tablets and went to work off my nut. I took a Lucozade bottle filled with gin and lemonade in to drink so I didn't feel the hangover kicking in which some would call a mender. I thought I would be able to fool people around me that I was sober, but they clearly saw differently, and I was sacked on the spot. Back to square one! So what did I do, I ended up taking a bar managers job in Sunderland town centre running one of the roughest pubs you can imagine. Drinking everyday was the norm, I'd swap pints for coke and be constantly getting lines shoved in my face.

Meeting My Partner

Then it happened, I met my amazing partner who at the time I judged and labelled because of all of the time he spent in the bar. One random night he asked me to go for a drink when the pub closed, and my guard was up. I didn't trust men because of my past situations and I always risk assessed everything around me. That was the best decision I ever made that night as I saw a beautiful, polite gentleman beneath the piss head I first saw in front of me. He was the start of a new beginning which I could have never predicted and showed me a happy way of life. As the relationship and love grew, the less alcohol he drank and less drugs I used. I didn't need that false reality anymore. I enjoyed being in the present seeing life through a different lens.

This was the start of my recovery and for once in my life, I was happy. Nothing was going to destroy it and take away my new beginning. I was very insecure, and my mental health was up and down like a roller coaster. This was more than just a quick fix. I needed support in different areas I had never even recognised because I had always put it down to the come down most the time. I referred myself into counselling services because I knew it was more complex. I didn't want to push away my new partner, so it was crucial I sorted myself out. When the substances became less, the clearer I saw and started to build confidence and strength within myself. This empowered me and I wanted a normal life like everyone else even more. The shame and the guilt started to slowly subside and pushed me to fight for more time with my children which was all I ever wanted. If I was close to them, I was winning, and they were the prize.

Abstinence

I have been substance free for 6 years this December I believe because for the first time in my life I found true happiness. I have a fantastic partner who is my soul mate. My mam always used to tell me one day you will meet your soul mate, and I thought she was talking absolute rubbish because of the shitbags I had been out with; I wouldn't have had another man gift wrapped! But it is so true. He has also battled demons in his life and that's what makes us special. We were two broken people and now we are whole, super cheesy I know but he is my best friend, and I appreciate him but most importantly we accept each other, flaws and all.

A Growing Family

In 2002 we had the biggest shock that could happen, I fell pregnant. My partner was told he couldn't have children because of testicular cancer so it was completely unexpected. I was so frightened; all the memories of the past came flooding back and I was terrified they were going to try and take my new baby away. If circumstances were different, I probably would have been overjoyed but your past never goes away, and I was so fearful and ashamed because I didn't want my partner to be subjected to parent assessments and all the crap that comes with the social.

At first it wasn't easy, but we showed resilience, strength and the love we had for each other and all our children was blinding for anyone to see. I changed my ways and my outlook on life before I became pregnant and that was evident for the local authority to see. We have 7 children and most recently 2 grandchildren to our bunch. The connection and family unit we have is priceless. I cherish every second of every day I get to spend with them and appreciate them all so much. If I have learned anything valuable in recovery it is not to take the people you love for granted or anything in life. I used to think I was a strong, confident young woman but looking back I wasn't. I was little girl who tried too much for people who didn't deserve her time or effort and that was all a front. I have learned to be humble, tolerant and that everything in life has a beauty. We just don't see it for the mist and the false sense of being addiction creates, you just have to keep fighting and looking for it. It is like hiding a flower from everything, but it needs to blossom, or eventually it will die. Guide it to the light and it will flourish and that's exactly what I have done.

Hope

In the chaos and the madness of my three-day benders and taking drugs until my heart came out of my chest, all I craved was someone to tell me it was all fixable and for someone to believe in me. When all hope is gone, you are defeated, what is there to fight for if you give up. Professionals tell you what you should be doing to be a better person, or an ideal parent but they had no idea of the torture and hurt that's ripping through you every time you open your eyes. Some days it was unbearable, and I would wake up begging for the pain to go away while my insides ached. I would do anything I could to get off my head for as long as possible, normally with alcohol first followed by a concoction of cocaine, crack then tablets to bring me down. How I am alive? I really do not know because I pushed myself to limits.

Stigma

I really struggled massively admitting to anyone that my children didn't live with me because of the sigma that mothers face who do not have their children. The expectation of a mother is completely different to a dad. Society and people label women brutally. I remember sitting in a lecture before I started working at Recovery Connections listening to student social workers talking about families and parents and I was mortified, I did not dare speak out. There were many times I had been bashed or feared for my life and I didn't ring the police because they just looked at me like the riff raff's girlfriend who deserves it for associating with scum bags. The police force especially a decade ago was very male dominated. Much worse than it is now and there was no sympathy whatsoever towards women. I was a victim of sexual assault, and I did not report it because of stigma from the professionals and anyone who found out about it. The stigma from the substances use didn't really bother me as much because I stigmatised and labelled myself. I viewed myself as a crack head who wasn't worthy of a good life or happiness and that's why I think I let myself become a punch bag for so many years. Social services have the power to destroy families and people's lives because of judgements and perceptions of what they read in the newspaper about people. I was told that it wasn't possible to change my life but how wrong they were! The system within society created barriers and challenges to me my whole life and now I work with many powerful people across the city. All the trauma I faced due to judgement has all been forgotten about because of the work I do; how would they feel if they read my history. I think there would still be judgement but I know I am a strong woman who will make change for other women.

Working for Recovery Connections now gives me the opportunity to go out everyday and spread the message of hope.

Yes, it is cheesy, but I believe that is what was missing from my life many years ago which would have made a huge difference for a motivation to change. Working with a Lived Experience Recovery Organisation makes going to work a blessing. We get it because we have been through it and know the raw emotion that some people will never feel. Our culture and values drive who we are, and people are my passion. Its crazy, public health and professionals think that I am the best thing since sliced bread because of my passion and honesty about how services operate. A few years ago, I was just the addict who lost her children whose opinion meant nothing. Now my voice means more than any professionals, yes I am an academic masters student but my lived experience is an asset that most people don't have. I have a voice, and I am not scared to use it for the best interests of others and for what's right.

A Woman of Substance Misuse

Emily Harold

My Life Now, Or Just for Today

Tonight, I finished work and got the train home. I had arranged my own journey and calculated the time I would need to leave the office to get to the train station. As I waited for the train, slightly anxious, I watched the passersby for whom this seemingly came second nature to. My train arrived and I jumped on, feeling very proud of myself. I hadn't missed it! I sat staring at the window, absorbed in the sights and watching as the sun was setting. It was beautiful and it filled me with so much warmth, joy and gratitude.

For an almost 40-year-old woman with 4 kids you might think, so what, big deal, people do this all day every day. But for me, someone who not that long ago, couldn't get out of bed, not even to wash or brush their teeth for days on end, it was a big deal! It was a huge deal and it filled me with so much pride in my journey, and not just the 30 minutes it took to get from work to home.

I have been in recovery for just over two years, and I now work within the recovery services. I live in the beautiful North Yorkshire countryside with my partner, three of my four children, two cats and a dog!

I love long walks, waterfalls, watching the sunrise and fall (cliché, I know!), foraging, wildflowers, making anything out of everything I find. Building dens and any bushcraft activity, just being a "*present*" parent for my children. Oh and of course, coffee!

However, my story hasn't always been this rosie, it took a dark turn, and I lost my way for a while. Let's rewind a couple of years.

Life With Conviction, Literally

"*I find the defendant guilty*!" (followed by the sound of the gravel bang!). Ok, so it might not have happened quite like that, but I have watched many true crime documentaries (I'm obsessed with those too!), that's how I imagined it to have happened. There I am, stood in a courtroom, tears streaming down my face, sporting a neck brace with a broken neck, possibly facing a prison sentence for a drink driving offence, and all that is going through my head is…I hope the local gazette isn't here reporting, I hope they don't print my name, take my photograph and publish my wrongdoings! What will my extended family think? What will my friends say? What will society and all those people behind a keyboard, people I don't know nor have met, write about me!? My life won't be worth living!! After all, I am a woman, a MOTHER!!!

Before getting into recovery, I was convinced there was a stigma attached to women with addiction, especially mothers. Women and mothers are portrayed to be nurturing, kind, superhumans who bring life into the world, manage juggling work commitments and childcare whilst maintaining a family home. And I strived to conform to such ideologies.

At the age of 21, I found myself a single mother still living with my parents. Before this, I had barely finished school, dropped out of college and university and to my wider family I was just a young mother who wasn't going to make anything of her life. And it was my aim to work my bloody socks off to prove them wrong!

I modelled myself on Barbra Taylor-Bradford's character in "*A Woman of Substance*". A young kitchen maid who overcomes poverty, relationship breakdowns and motherhood to become a wealthy and successful businesswoman. I worked long hours and studied part-time because, "*I wasn't going to rely on any man to look after me and my son*!" Or to quote the novel, "*We are each the authors of our own lives, Emma. We live in what we have created. There is no way to shift the blame and no one else to accept the accolades*".

So How Did I Get It So Wrong

For a time, this mindset and hard work paid off. I had a successful career, my own house, a new partner and a new baby. So where did it all go wrong? I remember coming home from work one evening, stressed and tired. The 6-year-old wanted his tea after a long day at breakfast club, school and after school club, the baby was screaming for a feed and the animals were going berserk around my feet to be fed too. I stood in the kitchen blank, not knowing who to feed first (seems like a minor stress doesn't it?). So, what did I do? I reached for a bottle of wine and fed my thirst for a release first.

Before I knew it, a glass after work turned into two, which then turned into a bottle which eventually led to me opening that second bottle. But that's ok, isn't it? We're allowed to, being a working mum? Mummy's "*wine*" down time, right?

This level of consumption lasted a few years, and I found myself scraping through each day, hungover, promising myself every Monday morning that I wouldn't have a drink that evening. However, by 11am I had already planned my trip to the shop before collecting the children.

My Most Important Relationship, Alcohol

I realised back then that my relationship with alcohol was turning sour. Why else would I google "*signs of a functioning alcoholic*"?

- [x] Constantly thinking about my next drink
- [x] Not being completely honest about my alcohol consumption (No Doctor/Dentist I do not consume more than 14 units a week! 😬)
- [x] Buying alcohol from different shops each day as to not be noticed by the cashiers
- [x] Buying a birthday card and gift bag with my wine to hide suspicion from cashiers (God, I was popular back then!)
- [ ] Drinking first thing in the morning
- [ ] Hiding alcohol
- [ ] Experiencing withdrawal symptoms

Please note, the above is not an accurate representation nor is it an "*How to Guide*" to avoid suspicion, believe me, it doesn't work! Anyway, I didn't tick all the boxes, yet, so I was safe, or so I thought, to continue my downward spiral and unhealthy relationship with alcohol.

Abuse and Misuse

Work events always involved alcohol, and lots of it. My glass was always full thanks to a male colleague who, on a number of occasions, took advantage of my impairment. I found myself unable to report these assaults, reasons being: He was in a position of power and authority so who was I to be believed? He paid my wages! I was drunk so of course it was my fault!?

It wasn't long before the effects of my alcohol consumption started affecting my day-to-day life, my anxiety was spiking and my mood dipping, my judgement at work was slipping and my relationship with my partner was breaking which in turn fuelled my thirst for more alcohol.

Home Life

Home life was becoming unbearable. My partner despised my eldest son from my previous relationship and the feeling was mutual. This led to my son leaving my family home. The family home I had worked so hard previously to build, to live with his dad. This broke me, really broke me! My relationship with my family fell apart, they blamed me for him leaving and so did I. I should have done more to make him stay, to make him want to stay with me but ultimately, I had to put his happiness and safety first and let him go. I had no one to turn to, my partner was happy he had gone, my family weren't talking to me, and I couldn't confide in my friends as this was admitting to them my failure as a mother. So, I turned to my next best friend, the friend that had been there over the years, who had helped me when I needed that release. Alcohol. But this time in the form of Gin. Neat Gin.

Trying to Do It On My Own

It wasn't long after I found out I was pregnant again with my third child. I immediately stopped drinking and worked on building my relationship with my family. All was going well until it wasn't. I had complications during my pregnancy. There was uncertainty around the pregnancy going full term and if it did whether the baby would be born healthy. This had an effect on my already declining mental health and my anxiety was reaching its highest point.

Lack of Help From Professionals

Forty weeks and eight days later, my third baby boy was born perfectly healthy and utterly beautiful. I was besotted again and felt truly blessed with this miracle baby. However, that didn't put an end to my anxiety, it continued on that steep peak. I was monitoring his every move, every flinch and every breath. I was convinced there was going to be something wrong with him, something that hadn't been picked up during the multiple scans and tests we had during pregnancy and after birth. Once he had reached all his newborn milestones and I was reassured he was ok, my anxieties turned to my own health. I diagnosed myself with throat cancer first, then bowel cancer and anything else DR Google told me. After all, anything could be possible after my history with alcohol I thought. I visited my GP on numerous occasions and was told "*it's all in my head* " and to "*stay away from Google*". I hadn't been honest about my past drinking habits as that would be admitting I had a problem and my failure as a mother, right?

I did as I was told and pushed through, fighting with this voice in my head. Until we visited a B&B on a night away for my son's sporting activity. The receptionist asked how old my baby was and proceeded to take note. Well of course some deep dark web of baby snatchers was going to snatch my baby whilst I slept! So I was going to make sure that there was no chance in hell of that happening! I barricaded all doors and windows, rearranged all furniture and laid awake all night grasping an empty wine bottle. I was ready for those baby snatchers! Of course, it didn't happen and I had a lovely Health Visitor who showed compassion and explained to me that this wasn't "*normal* " behaviour and I shouldn't be feeling such heightened anxiety. I was eventually diagnosed with Postnatal Depression and Health Anxiety and referred to the Perinatal team.

The Perinatal team didn't show such empathy as my Health Visitor had and I was told all these thoughts and anxieties were "*normal for a mother*" and "*it's just what us women have to deal with*". Well, I couldn't deal with it so clearly I wasn't "*normal* "!

As I always had done when times got tough, I turned back to my good friend, alcohol, for help. It didn't judge, it numbed all that noise in my head, and it helped me get some much needed sleep! Or so I thought.

Not long after, we entered lockdown, and my goodness wasn't that a great excuse for a binge? The first thing I did was order a box of 12 bottles of wine, that should last me a couple of weeks I thought. A few days later I was dry. I got thirsty earlier and earlier and before I knew it, I was supping on the dregs of wine from the previous night as soon as I woke.

I found out I was pregnant again during the second lockdown. Well what else was there to do?! And again, managed to curb my drinking habits. But that dark cloud was still hanging over me and as soon as my fourth son was born, I broke down. I hadn't left the hospital, and I was crying for help. I couldn't take it anymore. The midwives on the ward promised me they would put another referral into the Perinatal team and sent me on my way with a box of antidepressants. Well, this is where it gets a bit blurry, so bear with me. Nowhere to live, suicide and professional blunders…Within five weeks of my baby being born I had been kicked out of my home, my partner wouldn't let me see my children and I had made an attempt on my life.

I had ended up in hospital due to the suicide attempt and because of the visible bruises from the hands of my partner, social services, the police and the crisis team got involved. It became apparent that the referral from the hospital to the Perinatal team didn't happen. Could this have saved the rapid decline of my mental health and reliance on alcohol? Or would I have been faced with the same "*you just have to get on with it*" attitude. Who knows.

I wish I could say this event was enough for me to turn my back on alcohol for good. But the truth is, I was well and truly in the grip of addiction and still afraid to admit it. I was no longer functioning and ticked all the boxes and more.

Alcohol became my number one priority. I would wake up sweating and shaking, full of anxiety, dread and fear, craving the poison that would take it all away until the next day when the cycle started again.

A number of hospital visits, and a doctor looking at my stats, not me, telling me "*you are just someone who isn't going to be able to have a drink again*" but "*go away and reduce your alcohol intake*" didn't help me stop.

You'd think being kicked out of my home with nowhere to go and away from my children frequently would put an end to my drinking. Truth is, that fuelled it because I didn't want to feel everything I was feeling anymore. The shame, the hurt and embarrassment. My partner wouldn't allow me back into the family home and my parents couldn't cope with the responsibility of looking after me. During a stay at the hospital, they tried to organise a women's refuge for me, however children weren't allowed to stay or visit so this wasn't an option for me.

Continued Requests For Help Falling on Deaf Ears

After I finally took responsibility for my drinking and accepted I needed help, it still wasn't all plane sailing. On one occasion, my partner had taken me to a number of services to get help, but no one could offer me any support. I was sitting outside on the floor of their buildings because I was too weak to stand, crying, shaking and sweating due to withdrawals and still turned away.

The turning point in my story was when I was arrested for driving under the influence. I spent the night in a police cell and wasn't allowed to leave until I had sobered up. I finally did sober up, I sobered up right up until the night before my court date when I got so drunk due to the anxiety of the hearing the next day, I fell down the stairs and broke my neck. The scary thing is, I still have no recollection of this. It wasn't until I was laid in a hospital bed, isolated, staring at the ceiling, I thought "*sh*t, anything could have happened to me, I could be dead, and I wouldn't know. My children could be without a mother*". What kind of mother am I!?

Finding a Community of Like-Minded People

It was after this experience that I finally accepted my addiction and took responsibility for my own recovery. I found a community of like-minded people, people whose journeys I could relate to. A community with no prejudice. I realised that there is life after addiction, and I wanted to live that life!

In my first welcome meeting, I watched as a very professional and educated lady got her notes ready and I thought, oh here we go again, another medical professional telling me how bad alcohol is for my health and mental wellbeing… until she began to talk and speak of her 20+ years in recovery.

There is help out there and recovery is possible, and it is beautiful! We do recover and addiction does not define us.

Stigma still exists to this day, and I forget being surrounded by so much support in my community, but sadly it does. It exists in the wider community, within family and friendship groups and even within the NHS. And together with all the women in recovery, I am going to do everything in my power to break down these barriers for the women before us and the women who never got the opportunity to have a voice.

My Nanny would often tell me I would write a story about my life one day, but she would also tell everyone I stole her toilet paper in her dementia riddled rambles so of course I didn't believe her. But here I am telling my story, in hope that maybe one woman reading this may resonate and realise that she is not alone.

Hi my name is Emily, and I am an addict. I am also a woman and a mother!

P.S. I honestly didn't steal the toilet roll!

Conclusion: Women at the Epicentre of Change

Dr David Patton

Reading through the chapters within this book evoke a range of emotions as we gain such a deep and rich insight into the lived experiences of women navigating their recovery journeys. However, women's recovery experiences are not just testimonies of individual resilience but also powerful histories of the failures of existing services and systems. Throughout this book, we have seen how women navigate immense barriers - stigma, inadequate services, systemic violence, and a recovery landscape ill-equipped to meet their needs. Yet, despite these structural failures, the central truth that emerges from these narratives is not one of despair but of strength. Women do recover. More than that, and as I have written elsewhere, they are the transformative leaders of recovery, carving out spaces of healing, connection, and resistance, often in the very gaps left by failing institutions.[1]

This conclusion does not seek to repeat the barriers explored throughout this book but to shift the focus. Instead of fixating on what is broken, we must ask: Where is real change happening? And how can we cultivate more of it?

Looking in the Wrong Places: Why Systems and Services Cannot Be Our Focus

Addiction services, institutions, and policy structures have long been positioned as the primary mechanisms for addressing

1 Patton, D (2025) "*The Generative Culture of Recovery: the intersection of coloniality, utopian visioning and generative justice*", in Generative Justice: Beyond crime and punishment (Eds) McNeil, F. Corcoran, M & Weaver, B

substance use and recovery. Yet, as the lived experiences in this book reveal, these systems often do more harm than good. Services remain fragmented, cold and clinical, judgemental, punitive, and gender-blind, reproducing cycles of exclusion and stigma rather than facilitating meaningful recovery.

Women face unique and intersecting barriers that render mainstream recovery models inadequate. The fear of losing their children, the lack of trauma-informed care, the stigma of being an "*unfit mother*," and the absence of gender-responsive support all point to a fundamental failure of institutions to respond to women's needs.

Despite decades of research on gender-responsive treatment, the reality remains that services are not designed for women - they are designed around male models of addiction and recovery. Even where gender-specific services exist, they are often underfunded, inaccessible, or constrained by bureaucratic inefficiencies that limit their transformative potential.

If we continue to look to these broken systems for change, we will continue to be disappointed. The change we seek is not emerging from institutions. It is emerging from women and their communities.

Women as the Epicentres of Recovery

Recovery is happening in the spaces that women create for themselves and each other - within friendships, mutual aid networks, peer-led initiatives, and grassroots movements. These are the true epicentres of change. Women in recovery are building alternative structures of support that challenge institutional failures and replace them with lived-experience wisdom, collective care, and community-driven solutions.[2]

2 Ibid

These spaces are heterotopias - sites of resistance, healing, and possibility that exist outside dominant systems of control. They are places where women rewrite their own narratives, rejecting the identities imposed on them by stigma and trauma. Instead of being framed as "*damaged*" or "*deficient*," women in these spaces reclaim their strength, knowledge, and leadership.

Recovery is not just about ceasing substance use; it is about restoring self-worth, rebuilding trust, and fostering new ways of relating to the world. For many women, traditional services do not facilitate this; relationships, peer support, and community-based initiatives do.

Shifting Focus

If we accept that change is not emerging from institutions but from women themselves, then our focus must shift to cultivating more of these epicentres of recovery. How do we support the organic, community-led spaces where real transformation is happening?

1. Invest in Women's Leadership in Recovery

Women in recovery are already leading change, whether as mentors, advocates, or community organisers. Resources must be redirected toward supporting women-led recovery initiatives, ensuring that those with lived experience are positioned as experts and leaders rather than passive service users.

2. Develop Peer-Led, Community-Based Alternatives

Traditional treatment services often operate from a deficit model - viewing individuals in recovery as problems to be managed rather than as capable, knowledgeable agents of change. Instead, we need investment in peer-led and community-based recovery hubs that empower women to take control of their own healing.

3. Challenge the Structural Stigma Constraining Women's Recovery

Women in recovery face stigma not only from society but from within services themselves. Healthcare, social services, and criminal justice systems must be held accountable for perpetuating stigma and exclusion. Training and structural reforms must be implemented to ensure that women seeking support are met with dignity and respect.

4. Rethink Recovery Spaces

The future of recovery is not in clinical institutions but in lived-experience communities, holistic healing spaces, and grassroots initiatives. Recovery must be embedded in environments where women feel safe, seen, and supported.

5. Promote Economic and Social Empowerment

Recovery is not sustainable without economic stability and social inclusion pathways. Women in recovery need access to meaningful education, employment, housing and financial security. Policy shifts must address structural inequalities that leave women economically vulnerable post-recovery.

A Final Reflection: Shifting the Lens of Change

The lived experiences shared in this book reveal a simple but radical truth: Recovery is already happening, but it is happening in places we are not looking. Women in recovery are not waiting for institutions to change. They are creating their own pathways, their own networks of care, and their own models of transformation.

This conclusion is not a call for better services, though they are needed. It is a call for a fundamental shift in perspective. Instead of waiting for systems to catch up, we must recognise that the leadership, knowledge, and power needed to transform recovery already exist - within women and the communities they build.

Radical change will not come from the top down. It will come from the spaces women create for themselves, the connections they forge, and the new worlds they imagine into being.[3]

Our role is not to dictate what recovery should look like, but to listen, support, and amplify the voices of women who are already leading the way. The future of recovery does not belong to systems and services that have failed women. It belongs to women who are already leading the way. And it is happening now.

3 Levitas, R (2013), Utopia as Method: The Imaginary Reconstitution of Society. Palgrave MacMillan.

Printed in Great Britain
by Amazon

61715414R00112